16

995

THE BUDGET DEFICIT AND THE NATIONAL DEBT

Series Editor
Kenneth W. Thompson

Volume I
In The Miller Center Series on
The Budget Deficit and the National Debt

UNIVERSITY
PRESS OF
AMERICA

Lanham • New York • Oxford

The Miller Center

University of Virginia

Copyright © 1997 by
University Press of America,® Inc.
4720 Boston Way
Lanham, Maryland 20706

12 Hid's Copse Rd.
Cummor Hill, Oxford OX2 9JJ

Copublished by arrangement with
The Miller Center of Public Affairs,
University of Virginia

The views expressed by the author(s) of this publication do not necessarily represent the opinions of the Miller Center. We hold to Jefferson's dictum that: "Truth is the proper and sufficient antagonist to error, and has nothing to fear from the conflict, unless by human interposition, disarmed of her natural weapons, free argument and debate."

The budget deficit and the national debt / edited by Kenneth W. Thompson.
p.   cm. -- (The Miller Center series on the budget deficit and the national debt;
v. l)
l. Budget deficits--United States. 2. Budget--United States. 3. Debts, Public--United States. 4. Fiscal policy--United States. I. Thompson, Kenneth W. II. White Burkett Miller Center. III. Series.
HJ2051.B7713   1997 339.5'23'0973--dc21   97-3496 CIP

ISBN: 0-7618-0709-8 (cloth: alk. ppr.)
ISBN: 0-7618-0710-1 (pbk: alk. ppr.)

To

ALAN MURRAY

AND

JOHN BIRDSALL

Two who recognized the need for this Series

CONTENTS

I. THREE APPROACHES AND PERSPECTIVES

II. THE ORIGINS AND GROWTH OF THE DEFICIT AND THE DEBT

v

CONTENTS

III.   THE ECONOMICS AND POLITICS OF THE
DEBT AND THE DEFICIT

IV.   THE POLITICAL STRUGGLE FOR THE
DEBT AND THE DEFICIT

PREFACE

In October 1990, Senator Paul Laxalt participated in the Reagan oral history conducted by the Miller Center. His testimony sheds light on the changing attitudes of American leaders and the public toward annual federal deficits and the national debt. He recalled that when he joined the United States Senate, he brought with him certain rather traditional views concerning the national debt. Much as family debts that went on from year to year could be crippling, the nation's debt as it continued to mount annually would weaken and threaten solvency. As he continued in the Senate over the years, he was influenced by the prevailing view that family and national debt were not the same. In contrast with the family, the nation's solvency was undergirded by an array of factors that included a growing economy and national power that made comparisons with family resources problematic. Under the sway of Senator Hubert Humphrey and others, he recognized the prevailing view in the Senate that the national debt could sometimes have positive effects on the economy.

Today the opposite view appears dominant, although several of the contributors to the present volume challenge it in whole or in part (see in particular chapters 4 and 5). In the presidential election of 1996, the Republican candidate and his running mate for vice president proposed a substantial tax cut for the middle class. During the campaign, Senator Dole and Jack Kemp had less to say about the debt or about efforts to balance the budget than about a significant tax cut. If the writings of responsible columnists and the polls are accepted, the electorate turned out to care less about a tax cut than about continued efforts to balance the budget and reduce the debt. In other words, reducing the debt and the deficit for them had become more important than a tax cut, especially at a time when the economy was strong.

Thus it would seem that the people sensed, perhaps instinctively, the primacy of the budget and the debt as urgent problems on the national scene. For many of the reasons discussed by leaders and authorities in *The Budget Deficit and the National Debt*, it remains a critical problem. We embarked on our study because of widespread consensus on the urgency of the issues surrounding the budget. Some of the approaches paralleled the Center's primary focus on the presidency and governance. The budget is inescapably a case study in governance. The president is inevitably, at least most of the time, a key player in the submission of a budget and always in its approval or administration. The major processes of governance are engaged at every point in the discussions. Thus, the budget and the debt are appropriate subjects for study by the Miller Center. We have been extraordinarily successful in the speakers who have come to Charlottesville for these discussions. Through their explorations of the debt and the deficit, we are confident that all of us will gain a better understanding of the problem.

INTRODUCTION

Once having determined that the debt and the deficit were properly the business of the Miler Center, the question of how we should approach it arose. Debates in the Congress and the media highlight the importance of the assumptions observers bring to the question. The facts are frequently in dispute involving the Office of Management and Budget and the Congressional Budget Office. Political strategy and the quest for partisan advantage may drive the Republicans at one time to give priority to reducing the deficit or controlling the debt and the Democrats at another time.

Early on, we were committed to exploring, with representatives of different schools of thought, the variety of perspectives represented in the debate on the budget. The first three contributors provide differing frameworks for considering the subject. They provide the basis for the chapters that follow. A member of the Center's own governing council, *Wall Street Journal* bureau chief Alan Murray, was the logical choice to introduce the series. He had brought the budget, federalism, and the economy to the fore in Miller Center discussions. His view is that of an independent journalist. James Miller not only represents a different perspective, having served as director of the Office of Management and Budget in the Reagan administration; he is the recipient of a Ph.D. from the University of Virginia. He has sought high political office in the state expressing a conservative viewpoint. The perspective of mayors has figured prominently in discussions of the budget, especially in recent years. We were pleased, therefore, to have the mayor of Louisville, Jerry E. Abramson, contribute to the series, drawing on his three terms of office in that important city.

Another theme that runs through the debate over the budget has to do with the origins of the debt and the deficit and its growth and increase in various periods. Happily, Professor James Savage

ix

of the University of Virginia's Department of Government and Foreign Affairs is the author of the classic work on the subject. Savage brings long study and interest to the question. He points out that large-scale national debts were relatively unknown before 1932. He also questions whether solid evidence exists that reducing the deficit and the debt has some of the effects that are claimed for it. As the series progressed, we learned that Savage's *Balanced Budgets and American Politics* is highly regarded by a wide range of authorities. While not agreeing fully with Savage, George W. McKinney Jr., who at one time was senior vice president of Irving Trust, addresses some of the same problems. McKinney is Virginia Bankers Association Chair Professor Emeritus at the University's McIntire School of Commerce. He argues that many factors and variables, in addition to the deficit, affect interest rates as do other economic variables. He draws on Alfred Marshall's bowl of marbles to show how economic forces are in continual competition with one another as the economy moves toward a general equilibrium that represents an optimal position for the various economic forces. While Savage tends to emphasize the influence of political factors, McKinney concentrates more on economic factors as such.

The third contributor to the discussion of the growth of the deficit and debt is Larry Harlow. He traces the growth of the deficit as it occurred in the Bush administration. As a bureaucrat holding six senior governmental positions in the Reagan and Bush administrations and the son of the late Bryce Harlow, one of the nation's most revered theorist-practitioner who served in the Reagan and Bush administration, the younger Harlow identifies tactical and strategic errors that he maintains were devastating for the Bush tax increase. He holds that failure to keep Republicans in Congress and across the country informed was a "huge tactical mistake," as was launching summit discussions with too large a group from the Congress. Harlow recognizes that the United States had to show world leaders it was serious about deficit reductions so that they would stabilize interest rates. Thus, Harlow is critical, perhaps less of the Bush tax policy, than of the manner in which it was handled.

The final section in the volume addresses the economics and politics of the deficit. William Frenzel is a highly respected former congressman from Minnesota where he served as the ranking Minority member on the House Budget Committee and the main Republican economic spokesman in the House of Representatives. Frenzel begins by reciting facts: The deficit for some 23 years has averaged 4 percent of the gross domestic product; the debt has risen to $4.9 trillion; divided among 250 million Americans, each would owe approximately $20,000, an amount that is increasing every day. For him, Congress is the villain deserving two-thirds of the blame for our present straits. He attributes their actions to a "spend and elect" philosophy. In the last half-dozen years, Frenzel sees signs of change as the public feels threatened, and in 1994 it voted to "throw out" congressmen who ignored the deficit. He takes heart from the fact that Congress passed a budget resolution that seeks to balance the budget by the year 2002. Although some of the congressman's speculative "train wrecks" did not occur in 1995, the problem continues, but he remains hopeful, even on the politics of deficit reduction.

Robert Samuelson, columnist for *Newsweek* and the Washington Post Writers Group is one of the most widely read observers on governance and the economy. He traces the changes that have made the budget less a political document and more a tool of economic policy. He had expected that Congress and the White House would have agreed to balance the budget in the fall of 1995. Until the 1960s, a balanced budget was an instrument for defining the role and limits of government, establishing priorities and paying for these choices with appropriate taxes levied on the people. A balanced budget was a matter of political prudence and common sense. This prevailing attitude did not assure balanced budgets, particularly in times of war and economic decline. Before 1960, it provided a discipline for officials, however,but in the 1960s the discipline was lost as it became a tool for economic policy for improving the economy's performance, raising the rate of growth and sometimes altering the distribution of income. Thereafter, decisions on whether to have a deficit, balance the budget, or run a surplus had to be justified in economic terms. No consensus exists among the various theories on the effects of the budget on the economy. With no compelling economic reason to balance the budget, resulting in a political vacuum instead of a political framework, politicians do what is politically easiest: spend more and tax less, making deficits a permanent aspect of U.S. governance. Samuelson examines in turn the ideas of Sir Maynard Keynes, of investment for future social and economic benefits, and of supply-side economics but finds them all unconvincing nor, alternately, can he himself find convincing or measurable reasons for balancing the budget. In the face of these disappointing conclusions, Samuelson calls for the return of a viable political framework based on fiscal prudence as the most realistic constraint on an increasing deficit and debt.

David Maraniss is a Pulitzer Prize winning columnist and the author of an early biography on Bill Clinton. That book and a co-authored study of Speaker Newt Gingrich are two elements in Maraniss's chapter on the politics of the debt and the deficit. The politics of the struggle over the budget reflect the ambitions and rivalry of the two political figures. Maraniss sees the decision of Congressman Gingrich to shut down the government as occurring when Clinton rejected the seven-year Republican balanced-budget plan. Clinton reemerged as a relevant factor in disputes of this kind from a low point of November 1994. On 13 November 1995, Clinton refused to give in to the threat of an imminent government shutdown, and ultimately he prevailed. Maraniss chronicles the relation of the two key personalities as they fought for their views. The remainder of the chapter includes Maraniss's responses to detailed questions on the politics of the debt and the deficit, which help as much to explain the struggle as his earlier text.

I

THREE APPROACHES

AND PERSPECTIVES

« CHAPTER 1 »

THE BUDGET DEFICIT AND THE NATIONAL DEBT: A WALL STREET JOURNALIST'S INDEPENDENT VIEW*

ALAN MURRAY

NARRATOR: We are pleased that Miller Center Council member Dan Frierson, president of Dixie Yarn, Inc., in Chattanooga, Tennessee, could be with us today. Since he had a considerable role in attracting Alan Murray to join the Council, it is appropriate that he introduce our speaker.

MR. FRIERSON: Alan Murray is relatively new to the Miller Center Council but has a great deal of energy and enthusiasm. He was born in Akron, Ohio and raised in Chattanooga. He attended the University of North Carolina as a Morehead Scholar and received his master's degree from the London School of Economics. He began his career with the *Chattanooga Times* in 1977. In 1983 he moved to Washington and joined the *Wall Street Journal*, becoming its Washington bureau chief in 1992. He appears weekly on "NBC News at Sunrise," is a regular panelist in PBS's "Washington's Week in Review," and appears occasionally on other shows such as "Meet the Press" and "Sunday Times." He and

---

Presented in a Forum at the Miller Center of Public Affairs on 12 May 1995.

Journal reporter Jeffrey Birnbaum wrote *Showdown at Gucci Gulch: Lawmakers, Lobbyists, and the Unlikely Triumph of Tax Reform*, which received the American Political Science Association's Carey McWilliams Award.

The series of Forums we are embarking upon on the budget deficit and the national debt was largely his idea. It is a topic of considerable relevance to current political debate.

MR. MURRAY: The jokes people often tell about lying politicians reflect the enormous cynicism with which people in this country view Washington right now. In some ways the disdain Americans show for the government is the most shocking recent development in American public life. The Gallup Organization has been asking people for 40 years, "Do you trust your government in Washington to do the right thing all of the time or most of the time?" In 1963 about 75 percent of the people responding said "yes." Some of them said all of the time; the majority said most of the time. Today when people are asked that question, fewer than 20 percent say they trust our government to do the right thing all of the time or most of the time. The vast majority of the American people have grown so cynical about their own government that they believe most of the time it does more harm than good on balance. It is an extraordinary and discouraging development because democratic societies project their national identities to the world through their governments. Our current negativism reflects poorly on our national pride and self-image and has a debilitating effect.

There are many reasons why this attitude has developed over the past 30 years: the assassination of President Kennedy, the Vietnam War, Watergate, the inflation of the 1970s, and the Iranian hostage crisis. At least one contributing factor in the last 15 or so years has been the incredible disconnect between the way politicians talk about the budget deficit and the way they act. Both parties pay constant lip service to working toward a balanced budget, and yet both parties have almost completely failed to seriously address the deficit problem. Ronald Reagan, in his first address to Congress in 1981, said:

Can we who man the ship of state deny it is somewhat out of control? Our national debt is approaching $1 trillion. A few years ago I called such a figure—a trillion dollars—incomprehensible. I've been trying ever since to think of a way to illustrate how big a trillion is. The best I could come up with is that if you had a stack of $1,000 bills in your hand only four inches high, you would be a millionaire. A trillion dollars would be a stack of $1,000 bills 67 miles high.

By the time Ronald Reagan left office in 1989, that debt had more than tripled. The stack of $1,000 bills was over 200 miles high. The national debt was over $3 trillion. President Reagan's friends will tell you that the Democrats in Congress are to blame, but there is more than enough blame to go around to all sides. During the eight years that he was in office, President Reagan never submitted a proposal with specific measures designed to balance the budget. Likewise, neither President Bush nor President Clinton nor any of the responsible leaders in Congress during the last 14 years have ever submitted a proposal with specific measures aimed at getting the budget into balance. In fact, it was not until this very week that anyone in a position of responsibility had even pretended to submit a plan to bring the budget into balance. Thus, even though the two plans put on the table this week in the Senate Budget Committee and the House Budget Committee have plenty of holes and are vague in some areas, they are nonetheless extremely significant.

First, I would like to discuss briefly how we got to this position. Many people seem to think the United States has always run enormous budget deficits. That is not true. In the 150 years before 1932, the federal budget was in balance or surplus in two out of every three years, and for the most part the only time the United States ran deficits was during periods of war or immediately after a war. The American political system had a strong aversion to running deficits that emerged, like so many things in our system, from the debates between Hamilton and Jefferson. Hamilton was in favor of debt. He thought it healthy for the country to borrow and invest, that it would strengthen the country. Jefferson saw the debt issue in almost moral terms, however. He thought public borrowing was virtually the equivalent of public corruption, and said that "public debt was the greatest of dangers to be feared." In 1798 he wrote the following in a letter to his friend, John Taylor:

> I wish it were possible to obtain a single amendment to the Constitution. I would be willing to depend on that alone for the reduction of the administration of our government to the genuine principles of its Constitution. I mean an additional article taking from the government the power of borrowing.

In effect, he was calling for a balanced-budget amendment. He thought it was the one major omission in the Constitution.

Andrew Jackson, if anything, was even more adamantly opposed to public borrowing than Jefferson was. To eliminate the debt remaining from the War of 1812, he ran huge surpluses, announcing that the United States now set "the rare example of a great nation, abounding in all the means of happiness and security, altogether free from debt."

There were similar circumstances after the Civil War. The Republicans were determined to get rid of the wartime debt as quickly as possible, and in fact did so. A British diplomat who was visiting the United States at the time thought that this obsession was a little strange, and wrote back to England that "the majority of Americans would appear disposed to endure any amount of sacrifice rather than bequeath a portion of their debt to future generations. There is in the American character a strong and controlling sense that debt was always and everywhere an evil."

Even in 1932 when Franklin Roosevelt was first running for president, he attacked Herbert Hoover for running deficits and promised to balance the budget. He of course failed to do so, in part because the economy was in such miserable shape.

The pivotal change in Americans' thinking about deficits resulted from the ideas of John Maynard Keynes. Prior to his arrival, most economists had simply elaborated the essential wisdom of Adam Smith's *The Wealth of Nations*, believing that an invisible hand operated in capitalist economies and that the economy would correct itself. Keynes argued persuasively that in some circumstances this process does not work—as in the case, for example, in which people are not spending money because they do not have jobs, causing companies to lay off more people who, in turn, also do not spend money. He said the only way to break that vicious cycle would be for the government to step in and spend borrowed money to bring the economy back to health.

That idea really did not have much influence on the Roosevelt administration. Roosevelt met Keynes once and did not care for him at all. He told Frances Perkins, his labor secretary, that Keynes seemed a little wacky. Keynes did not care much for Roosevelt either and thought that he was unsophisticated about economics. Not until World War II did government spending increase enough to have a significant stimulating effect on the economy, and it was not until after the war that the ideas of Keynes became common-place, at least in Democratic administrations. By the time of the Kennedy and Johnson administrations, Keynesian-trained econo-mists enjoyed considerable influence in the executive branch, offering advice on how to use budget deficits to spur the economy in times of weakness. Americans had so much confidence at the time that they thought they had largely overcome recessions. In the late 1960s there was a government publication called *Business Cycle Digest* whose name was changed to *Business Conditions Digest* because people thought business cycles had ended and we were not going to have any more recessions. That incident demonstrates the confidence that Keynes' ideas inspired in Democratic adminis-trations.

The Republicans, of course, never quite accepted this notion. Eisenhower was devoted to achieving a balanced budget, as were many Republicans in Congress. The Republicans thus imparted to the political system a certain level of discipline until the advent of "supply-side economics" in the late 1970s.

Supply-side economics differed in its origins from Keynes-ianism. It was not born in academia. An economist named Art Laffer left his position at the University of Chicago, worked in the Office of Management and Budget, and put together a wildly opti-mistic budget forecast that was ridiculed in Washington and by his friends in academia. Paul Samuelson, the economist at MIT, revealed in a speech in Chicago that Laffer, who had been granted tenure at Chicago, had never quite finished his Ph.D. requirements at Stanford University. A huge scandal ensued, and Art Laffer grew very depressed. His marriage broke up and he began putting on a lot of weight.

About that time—the early 1970s—he met the other person who was instrumental in founding supply-side economics, a journalist by the name of Jude Wanniski. Wanniski was the son of a coal miner. His grandfather was a Lithuanian emigré and a socialist. When Jude Wanniski was young, he accompanied his grandfather to some socialist meetings. He started his journalism career in Las Vegas and arrived in Washington in the late 1960s with his new bride, a Las Vegas show girl, and was given a job by Dow Jones, my own organization, at the *National Observer*. Realizing that economics was becoming more important in the world and in the United States, he decided to find a tutor for himself. He read about this scandal surrounding Art Laffer, decided that he would probably be the right person to tutor him in economics, and approached him. Laffer was lonely, and the two of them became very close and spent hours together talking about economics.

Wanniski was most impressed by the notion that there is a tax rate that the government cannot exceed, or it will begin to lose revenue. For example, if tomorrow I tell everyone that their income will be taxed 100 percent, the odds are that they will not go to work, and I will not collect much money. Clearly, one can reach a point where taxes are so high that they discourage work, resulting in lost revenue. Wanniski, an enthusiastic fellow, immediately leaped to the conclusion that the United States had already reached that point. Therefore, by cutting tax rates, the U.S. government could raise *more* revenues, and we would not have to worry about the budget deficit anymore. By simply cutting taxes the government would encourage people to work more and thereby bring in more money, and everything would be fine.

No real evidence existed to back up this theory, except at the highest end of the scale. People who were in the 70 percent bracket might have been motivated to earn more money or at least report more of their earnings if the rate were somewhat lower, and therefore the government could bring in more revenue from those people. There was no evidence, however, to suggest that cutting tax rates for the vast middle class could somehow lead to more revenue being collected. Thus, from the very beginning the economics were shaky, but the politics were very appealing to Republicans, who were in a mess after Watergate.

Jude Wanniski wrote a compelling article called "The Two Santa Claus Theory." He said that Democrats had been winning elections because they played the role of Santa Claus in giving out government spending programs. The Republicans would insist on balancing the budget, arguing that we had to raise taxes to pay for these programs. As long as that is the dynamic, the Democrats will win. Wanniski said the country needed to have *two* Santa Clauses. The Republicans ought to say, "OK, the Democrats can give you spending programs; we will give you tax cuts." It would thus be Christmas 365 days a year.

That idea caught the attention of a politician named Jack Kemp. At first it was ridiculed within the Republican party, but by 1978 the party leaders were desperate, so they embraced the Kemp-Roth tax cut proposal. This paved the way for a few new Republican members of Congress to be elected in 1978, one of whom was a man from Georgia by the name of Newt Gingrich. By 1980 they had sold Ronald Reagan on this proposal, and the Republicans were elected to office on the basis of this supply-side theory. In 1981, a bidding war for huge tax cuts occurred, with no one paying much attention to the spending cuts that would have been necessary to offset those tax cuts. The result is history. Our country went from deficits in the range of $40 or $50 billion to deficits of $200 billion a year, and the national debt soared from less than $1 trillion to almost $5 trillion today.

Why should anyone care about deficits? That is a reasonable question to ask, since the 1980s were not so bad. Some economists in 1980 and 1981 warned that if this huge tax cut were enacted, massive budget deficits would result, which would lead to rampant inflation. The United States did in fact have massive budget deficits but *not* rampant inflation. Inflation stayed at about 4 percent during the middle and late 1980s and is at 3 percent now. Other economists forecast that the tax cuts would eventually prompt a huge recession. In the 1980s, the United States had one of the longest economic expansions in modern history. It created millions of jobs at a time when European countries were creating no jobs. A recession did occur in 1990 in our country, but it was fairly mild by historical standards, so that prediction seemed to be totally untrue as well.

It is therefore quite reasonable to ask at this point, 15 years later, "Who Cares?" What price are we paying for these budget deficits? The reason that this question is so hard to answer convincingly in a manner people can understand was best put by Charlie Schultz, who served in the Carter administration and is now an economist at the Brookings Institution. He says that the way deficits affect the economy is not like a wolf knocking at the door; it is more like termites eating at the foundation. It is a slow corrosive effect, and it only hits over a long period of time.

A basic rationale explains how deficits hurt the economy. As a country, we in the United States save very little compared to most of the other major economies in the world. Our national savings rate is 4.8 percent and has been about the same for many years. Japan saves almost four times as much as we do on average, while Germany, France, and Canada all save more of their income as well.

When the government needs money, it appropriates it from this pool of national savings. That is the money available for borrowing. Most of what we have saved during the 1990s was used to finance the government's budget deficit. If our country existed alone in the world, that would mean that only 1.8 percent of our national income would be available for private companies to raise capital, and private investment would be squeezed. In theory that would bid up interest rates, thereby either prompting people to save more or prompting companies to invest less, thus yielding a rough equilibrium.

The United States, of course, is not alone in the world. American companies borrow from foreign capital markets, and in the 1980s we found them doing so quite freely. Economic theory teaches that overseas borrowing carries a somewhat higher interest rate because it is more difficult and risky than investing in the domestic market. This, in turn, drives up domestic rates. These higher interest rates discourage investment, at least in theory. Investment is critical to the productivity of American workers. If a farmer cannot buy a tractor, it will take him much longer to till his field. If workers are less productive, they cannot be paid as much, which ultimately means a stagnant standard of living. That is the theory.

What actually happened? First, the amount of domestic investment per worker in the United States dropped to a level considerably lower than that of other major countries. That situation seems to fit pretty well with the theory. Moreover, the productivity growth of American workers in this country has been considerably lower since 1973 than it was before then. In the two preceding decades, the productivity of American workers had been growing 3 percent every year. This was the golden age of the American economy—more cars in the garage, more appliances in the kitchen. On average, American living standards were doubling every 25 years. In the period since 1973 productivity has grown at an annual rate of only 1 percent. This shows that a dramatic change has taken place in the American economy over the last 20 years. The average worker in America today could be earning $19,000 more than he or she presently is if the productivity growth rate that existed before 1973 had continued.

Did the budget deficit cause this slow growth? That is hard to say, particularly if one looks at the timing. Budget deficits were not that big in the 1970s, and other factors certainly influenced economic conditions. The first oil shock occurred in 1973, driving up inflation. Surely, that circumstance must have something to do with the poor performance in the 1970s and 1980s. The conventional economic wisdom, however, whether right or wrong, suggests that the growth and persistence of huge budget deficits in the 1980s has something to do with this productivity gap.

What makes this gap even more disturbing is that some people have done just fine over the last 20 years, particularly people who have college educations or the necessary skills for our high-tech economy. The people who have been really hit hard are those who do not have a college degree. Perhaps 15 or 20 years ago they could have gotten a high-paying job at an auto factory or a steel factory, but those jobs no longer exist. We hear a great deal today about the volatility of angry young men in our political system. Those people are angry for a reason: They are the ones who have gotten the raw end of this economic deal and have seen their

11

earning power decline over the last 20 years. Their resentment has been exacerbated by such social policies as affirmative action. Some men in society today worry about the rising status of women. If you look at the people who voted Democratic in 1992 and Republican in 1994, it tends to be just those people—largely white, largely male, largely people with no college degree. I think one can make a strong argument that their economic predicament presents the greatest challenge faced by the American society and economy today.

What can we do about this situation? First, it is important to note that unlike every president before him in the postwar era, Bill Clinton was really the first president who was primarily focused on economics. He was the first true post-Cold War president. Having come from the state of Arkansas where this problem of impoverishment was magnified, he was accustomed to dealing with these conditions. As a result, during his campaign he articulated a fairly clear vision of how to address this problem of stagnating earnings and living standards. The *Atlantic Monthly* referred to that vision as the "Field of Dreams Theory" of economic development, after the movie of the same name where the voice whispered, "If you build it, they will come." The notion was that in today's global economy, tax breaks or subsidies for business are useless because the fungibility of money allows businesses to take the money and invest it overseas in Malaysia or Taiwan. Then-governor Clinton argued that the way to attract business to the United States is to build up public infrastructure by making key government investments. He saw an important role for the government in bolstering such areas as education, training, telecommunications, and technology so that the best companies in the world with the best jobs would want to locate here. It is not unlike what states do all of the time in promoting development. That was policy number one.

Policy number two was getting rid of the budget deficit. There was a bit of conflict between those two goals, however, and Clinton never really successfully addressed that dilemma during or *after* the campaign. How does one pay for all of these public investments when a $200 billion deficit exists? Theoretically, there are two ways to do it. First, one can raise taxes, which is not the most politically popular thing to do. President Clinton was willing to raise taxes on people at the top end of the income scale, but not on the middle class. Second, one can cut spending on those programs that do not qualify as public investment. Social Security, Medicare, Medicaid, farm programs, and veteran programs all fall into this category but are immensely popular with key parts of the electorate. President Clinton, of course, never had the inclination or the will to go after those programs. Thus, the economic strategy that he articulated throughout the campaign never materialized. Congress would not appropriate the money for major new investments. Clinton made some progress at reducing the deficit, but not very much. By the 1994 election, the perception had taken hold, partly because of the health care plan and the way he handled gays in the military, that Clinton really was not a New Democrat at all, that he was instead a traditional Democrat big spender. People were fed up with it, so they turned to the Republicans in droves.

I spent a fair amount of time on the road in 1994 trying to get some sense of what that election was all about. Without question, there were many angry people out there. Nevertheless, it was hard to find a coherent debate about the fundamental economic questions that supposedly fueled this discontent. I went to Tennessee, which was in some ways the hotbed of the Republican revolution—it had two Democratic senators before the election and two Republican senators afterward. Three Tennessee Democratic incumbents in the House of Representatives were defeated by Republicans. The incumbent governor was a Democrat; his replacement was a Republican. Clearly, the voters in Tennessee were angry people. Interestingly, however, no one talked about the Contract with America. No one knew what it was! The kinds of things that were discussed were trivial. Senator Sasser accused his opponent, Bill Frist, of having cut up little cats when he was in medical school. That was one of the big issues. Bill Frist then said during one of the debates, "Senator Sasser, during the time that you have been in office, illegitimate births have increased threefold." Senator Sasser did not know how to respond, and he is now out of office. At any rate, we ended up with this revolution that is now taking place in Washington.

The Contract with America does indeed represent a dramatic change in the direction of national policy, but in my view it is

13

nothing compared to what happened this week. The House Budget Committee and the Senate Budget Committee both laid reasonably specific plans on the table for balancing the federal budget by 2002. They are somewhat trapped by their own rhetoric on this issue because for months they have been telling us that accomplishing a balanced budget would not be particularly painful. Spending does not really have to be cut, they claim; just increase it a little more slowly. Anyone who draws up budgets for anything recognizes that inflation has to be taken into account. Over a seven-year period, spending would have to increase by about 23 percent just to keep up with projected inflation. Health care, which takes up so much of the federal budget, has a 10 percent annual inflation rate, so it requires much bigger increases to keep up with inflation. There is obviously a huge difference between the amount of money the government would have to spend to maintain its current level of services compared to the amount the Republicans now propose to be spending by 2002.

To illustrate how dramatic this change is, the total combined annual sales of Texaco, Chrysler, IBM, Sears, and DuPont roughly equal the size of the net budget reduction in 2002. It would be like eliminating all five of those corporations. Such a dramatic turn in direction does not normally occur in American government. The reason the cuts are so big is because the deficit is so large and because the Republicans are only going to deal with it on the spending side and do not want to raise taxes. In the House of Representatives, on top of that, they have to make additional spending cuts to "pay for" a tax cut that will cost $350 billion over the next seven years. We are talking about a major downsizing of government.

One of the most dramatic examples is spending on foreign aid and international affairs. It is not popular, and no one likes to do it. However, the United States already spends far less in relative terms than most of its trading partners. The United States spends about 1 percent of its budget, or $18 billion a year in this area. Just to keep up with inflation, that would have to increase to $22 billion a year. The House Budget Committee is proposing that the United States spend only $10 billion a year, which would be a 60 percent drop in spending on foreign aid and international affairs. These are huge changes.

It is hard to think of any time in U.S. history when there have been such diametrically opposed visions of how to deal with a given problem. We have a president who says the way to deal with it is to first spend more money on public investments such as education, training, technology, and infrastructure. Meanwhile, we have a leadership in the House of Representatives that says the way to deal with it is to get rid of the budget deficit and get government out of the way. They are cutting education and training and eliminating President Clinton's technology programs as well as the so-called investments such as Head Start and other programs that President Clinton argues are necessary to deal with this problem. The two sides have come to opposite conclusions. There is clearly a grain of truth in both positions, and the only way to reconcile them is through tax increases and cuts in the politically sensitive entitlement programs. Neither party is willing to address either of the issues.

In spite of the fairly extreme positions taken by politicians on either side, the American people are still squarely in the middle, where they have always been. According to the polls, President Clinton has not recovered in popularity since the November election, although his popularity did bounce up a bit after the April 1995 tragedy in Oklahoma City. Speaker of the House Newt Gingrich has gone steadily down in the polls and is not very popular. His views are too extreme and he now has higher negative ratings than those of the President. The person who has benefited from all of this is a person who has not done much of anything this year: Senate Majority Leader Bob Dole. He could not get a balanced-budget amendment through the Senate, nor could he get his regulatory relief bill through the Senate. He has not been very successful in leading the Senate. Yet simply by virtue of being between those two polar forces (Clinton and Gingrich), his numbers are shooting up in the polls, and that gives a pretty clear indication of where the American people are.

As a footnote to this discussion, it is ironic that the President and the Speaker of the House personally seem so similar, despite their enormous differences of opinion. They both are about the same age. They both are baby boomers with no military experience.

They both seem to thrive in an atmosphere of chaos and inefficiency. They both had very bizarre and tense relationships with stepfathers and extraordinarily close relationships with their mothers. One of President Clinton's finest moments this year came after Newt Gingrich's mother had the infamous interview with Connie Chung and called Hillary Clinton a witch, or whatever it was. President Clinton answered a reporter's question about that at a photo opportunity by saying, "Well, just imagine if Connie Chung had gotten hold of *my* mother!" Finally, they both seem to be fighting a losing battle against their expanding waistlines. The joke about President Clinton is that he had one of these thousand dollar a plate fund-raising dinners and lost money because he ate so much. The joke about Newt Gingrich is that he wants to stop delivering school lunches so he can have them himself. I find it interesting that these two men who seem to have so much in common have brought such severe polarization to government.

QUESTION: For a long time the conventional wisdom in Washington held that real deficit reduction would only occur when the president and Congress worked together and the Democrats and Republicans worked together in private, as they did in the old Social Security reform commissions. Reduction was also said to require a compromise package of some revenue increases and some spending cuts. Is any of that still true?

MR. MURRAY: You are correct in saying that the assumption in Washington for some time was that the deficit problem could only be addressed on a bipartisan basis with everything being put on the table, including Social Security. Approximately 50 percent would be tax increases, and approximately 50 percent would be spending cuts.

In spite of budget summits and so forth, progress in addressing the big problem has been very limited. What is extraordinary is that the Republicans are taking such a high-risk, go-it-alone approach. They are doing it with no changes in Social Security and no increase in taxes, so the job is much, much more difficult. Under their highly partisan style, one party takes all of the heat for the reforms.

The one thing that has changed which gives this effort at least a fighting chance is the zealous attitude of the new members of

Congress, which reflects the attitude of the public. I have spent a great deal of time talking to these freshmen and sophomores of Congress, who now account for half of the House of Representatives. These people are almost messianic in the way they talk about this problem—"By God, we're different; you guys have messed this up for a decade. We promised people we were going to deal with it; it's a solemn promise; we're not career politicians; we came here to deal with this problem and we're going to do it and we don't care what the ramifications are." I'm not sure they really know what the ramifications are, but their zeal is extraordinary and unlike anything that existed in 1981.

That new spirit reflects a change in the public—the enormous cynicism people now have. Even though the Republicans are locked into this tax cut position because they promised to do it, they will not receive much political benefit for it because the public is so cynical. When a politician says "I'm going to cut taxes," people immediately assume he or she is just pandering to get votes rather than doing something for the good of the country. That cynicism has bred this new class of members of Congress who change the dynamic rather dramatically. They are not a majority, so they cannot pass a budget and all of these appropriations bills by themselves. Come November, however, Congress will have to vote to raise the debt limit in order to prevent a default. The debt limit right now is $4.9 trillion. If Congress does not increase it, the nation will default for the first time in history. The government would not be able to pay Social Security checks; it would not be able to meet its debt obligations. It is a serious thing. Those freshmen and sophomores will have to vote to increase that debt limit, and they are saying unequivocally that they will not cast that vote until firm, enforceable, specific measures are put in place to get a balanced budget by 2002. I do not know what will happen, but it is going to be an interesting six months.

QUESTION: You have not mentioned anything about the impact of the large lobby groups, in particular the American Association of Retired Persons (AARP) on the debate over health care costs and Social Security, which are the biggest budget items. I wonder if these zealous freshmen and sophomores in Congress really know what they are up against.

MR. MURRAY: Three months from now, they will. One member of Congress said to me, "I admit we haven't had angry ladies banging on our cars with umbrellas yet. We'll see what happens when it does." That is an interesting question. I do not want to oversell what was put on the table this week. While it does call for big cuts in Medicare, both the Senate Budget Committee and the House Budget Committee flinched from putting down specific proposals for achieving them.

QUESTION: In the real world of economics and politics, what are the best ideas that you have heard—not necessarily your own—to solve this dilemma?

MR. MURRAY: One of the great things about being a journalist is that you do not have to formulate any solutions. It is like being Ross Perot in the presidential race. As I tried to suggest earlier, I think there is a grain of truth in what both parties are saying. I think it is important that we balance the budget to deal with this fundamental problem of stagnating living standards. I also think it is a good idea to put some carefully targeted, smart public investments in such areas as education. The big class gap that exists in this country today is between people who have college degrees and people who do not, and it is widening. Therefore, investing federal money in education, training, and technology—as President Clinton is talking about—makes some sense.

The question is, how can both things be done at once if we are not willing to raise taxes? We can only do that if we are seriously willing to take on the entitlement problem, and that includes Social Security. My next statement is going to get me into all kinds of trouble, but we have a situation in the country today where a person struggling to raise a family with a couple of kids on $30,000 a year loses about 15 percent (counting both employer and employee deductions) that is deducted from every paycheck for the benefit of someone who, on average, is already better off than that working family. I am certainly not saying that Social Security should be eliminated, but it seems to me that there is some action we could take—for instance, means testing. When the Social Security system was put into place, the average American did not live much beyond 65 years of age. Medical science has changed that dramatically for the better, which is great, but perhaps the Social Security retirement age should be gradually raised.

LINWOOD HOLTON: Do you think that is really the answer? The cuts proposed by Senator Domenici this week are going to make "the great middle" realize that not just a quantity of dollars is at stake. These cuts mean that "out of pocket" costs for medicine will increase. That is going to irritate middle America, but those people will eventually realize, probably before the politicians, that if one wants these benefits, one has to pay for them. There are politically acceptable ways to increase taxes as long as the results of cuts are made apparent. The age at which people begin receiving Social Security can be increased. I am seven years beyond the basic Social Security retirement age, and I am still working! Nevertheless, I receive a check every month, whether I want it or not. It is silly! It is also true that I do not have to report all of it for income taxes, and that is silly. People will consent to increased taxes after they find out what these cuts mean.

For example, people think about foreign aid as dollars, but it is mostly about jobs in the United States because foreign aid goes to buy airplanes or bullets made in the United States. When those workers get laid off, they are going to realize what a cut in foreign aid means. When the effects of those cuts become apparent, I think that the American public will go back to the old-fashioned way: Pay as you go. It was not so long ago, when I was governor of Virginia, that if one wanted to clean up the rivers, taxes were raised to pay for it. No one objected to that approach. I do not think the cynicism will prevail when the middle American sits down and realizes what the full ramifications are.

COMMENT: The Kerrey-Danforth Committee developed a piece of software called "entitlement" that tests various minor budget modifications to see what their cumulative effect would be on the deficit. It is a very discouraging exercise. All of the things about which we have talked, such as raising the Social Security age to 70, that seem to be politically unacceptable now do not add up. There would have to be a startling change to balance this budget.

MR. MURRAY: I do not have the exact numbers, but raising the Social Security retirement age to 70 would save a fair amount of money. At least it is a good start. We will certainly have to deal with Medicare. Social Security and defense used to be the biggest parts of the budget, but Medicare is passing them, leaving them both in the dust with at a growth rate of 10 percent per year. A solution to the Medicare and Medicaid problems must be found. Otherwise, as the next century arrives, health care costs will be eating up half of the government's budget. It really would not be that hard to control, however. A 25-cents-per-gallon gasoline tax would make some real progress! We are a very rich nation, and we can afford to do this, either through spending cutbacks or through tax increases. It is not that difficult.

QUESTION: You talked about the reasons for declines in productivity. Throughout the 1950s and 1960s, our country had a highly unionized labor force that could raise its wages virtually at will just by holding strikes. The more companies pay out in labor costs, the less they have in retained earnings available for reinvestment. What was the role of union labor in America's declining productivity? It seems that the steel industry priced itself out of the market, as did the auto industry. Now in Virginia we have textile plants that are closing down.

MR. MURRAY: I do not have a complete answer. There is not nearly as much union power today as there was 15 years ago. Yes, one can argue that unions priced themselves out of the market, but one can also argue that the car and the steel companies let them do it because they did not recognize the changes in the world market in which they were operating. The only thing I can say is that the share of total national output going to labor and the share going to corporate retained earnings have not changed much over time. Individual industries and companies may have high labor costs problems, but I do not think it has a big effect on the national numbers. Nationally, the bottom line is, people will be paid more if they are more productive over time.

QUESTION: You discussed the lack of increases in productivity that beset America for a prolonged period of time, but in the last couple of years that trend has changed. What has been the cause for this change?

MR. MURRAY: There has been a big productivity increase in manufacturing, but not in the service sector, which accounts for an ever greater share of the economy. I think the explanation is increased use of computers, although this is a guess. It seems as though the computer technology revolution took off a decade or more ago, but there has been a fairly slow learning curve. Everyone bought computers without knowing quite what to do with them. I can certainly see that in the offices in which I have worked. We had not learned how to use this incredible tool to increase productivity until fairly recently. In the last couple of years, there have been signs that overall productivity has begun to inch up. It may not return to the 3 percent annual growth rate of the 1950s and 1960s, but it should be considerably better than the 1 percent trend of the 1970s and 1980s.

QUESTION: Concerning Medicare, will we see such changes as the restriction of doctors' salaries, lowering the profits of pharmaceutical companies, or the introduction of tort reform? These changes are politically unpopular and may be economically counterproductive.

MR. MURRAY: As you know, most efforts to get Medicare costs under control have focused on pushing down reimbursements to doctors and hospitals. That is politically easier to do than cutting benefits. Some of the people working on these Republican plans now discuss trying to encourage people to join health maintenance organizations (HMOs) and managed care plans that will save the government money. Corporations have been remarkably successful in the last year or two at getting people into managed care programs and thereby saving money. The government wants to do the same thing, so it is going to try to encourage people to move into an HMO by increasing out-of-pocket expenses if one chooses not to be part of an HMO. Speaker Gingrich says the Republican plan would not force people into an HMO. These are the changes presently being talked about. I do not know how much money could be saved as a result of these changes, but they represent a start.

QUESTION: As a result of all of this confusion and turmoil, will the Republican steamroller be stopped in November?

MR. MURRAY: Since this Medicare issue popped up recently, many more smiling faces have been seen at the White House than there were six months ago. The Republicans rode the public's cynicism into office, but now they have to deal with it themselves, and they have gotten themselves in a real bind. In fact, they know that if they do not make these cuts, they will lose because they repeatedly made a solemn promise to do so in the strongest of terms. The American people would say, "What good are you? You're no better than the last guys." If they *do* fulfill their promise, however, they may lose anyway. The argument they make is, "At least if we do it, there is a chance people might like it, and maybe we'll survive." I would not begin to predict which party will win the presidency in 1996.

In June 1992, I was with a panel of *Wall Street Journal* journalists, including Karen Elliott House; Al Hunt, who at that time was the Washington bureau chief; and Paul Gigot, the Washington columnist for the editorial page. This was only five months before the 1992 election, and someone asked, "Who's going to win?" All of us said George Bush, except for Al Hunt, who said Ross Perot.

QUESTION: Since a great deal of our public debt is held by investors who live in foreign countries and since the global economy is being rapidly developed by GATT and similar agreements, we are becoming more dependent on events abroad. How do you as an economist look at that trend in relation to the balanced budget?

MR. MURRAY: It leaves us in the position of Blanche du Bois in *A Streetcar Named Desire*—we are rather dependent on the kindness of strangers. We saw in Mexico the potential dangers of being so heavily reliant on foreign money—if it comes in and is then stopped, it can leave a country in a mess. Fortunately, we are a long way from being Mexico. Fluctuations in the willingness of investors to hold the dollar can cause fluctuations in interest rates, but they are relatively small in scale. There is no sign yet that the world isn't willing to lend the United States all of the money it wants to borrow.

QUESTION: What are your opinions about a national sales tax or a consumption tax? Also, if Congress does pass a budget bill that the President signs which does even half of the dramatic things they are proposing, what will be the effect on the states and our taxes?

MR. MURRAY: First, tax reform is not something that will be seriously addressed before the election. The Republicans are building it up as an issue for the election campaigns. Republicans have won the presidency in the post-World War II period with basically two arguments. One is the fight against communism, but there is no communism left to fight; the other issue is tax cuts. Since they are trying to balance the budget by 2002 and have already promised a bunch of tax cuts, they cannot promise much more. Thus, tax reform is an attempt to find a substitute for tax cuts.

Dick Armey has proposed not a national sales tax, but a flat-rate personal income tax—17 percent. Although his proposal sounds very appealing, it has a couple of major flaws. One is that it does not raise nearly enough money. A rate closer to 23 percent in the Armey plan would be needed to raise as much money as the current system does. Second, implementing a flat tax would cause a major redistribution of the tax burden. The people at the bottom of the income scale would do OK because they are exempted, and the people at the top get a big tax cut. Those people in the middle who have been getting the raw end of the economic deal for the last 20 years would get a tax *increase*, however. Politically, I do not think that will sell once people see the details.

23

In the Senate, Pete Domenici and Sam Nunn have proposed a novel plan to increase savings, which I emphasized is crucial for financing investment and boosting productivity. They called for a tax system that encourages savings by not taxing them—just like having giant IRAs. All of the money put aside for savings and investing will not be taxed. However, they intend to raise as much money and be as progressive as in the current tax system; that is, the same distribution of the burden. It is an attractive concept; in fact, however, a tax rate of 40 percent would have to be imposed all the way down to those people making $40,000 or $50,000 a year. That would be a big increase in the tax rate. The money that people spend would have to be taxed to provide this big tax break for the money that people save. People who saved a lot would be better off, but people who did not save would be worse off. Politically, that is an empty proposition.

The sales tax Senator Richard Lugar has proposed is in some ways the most radical idea, not unlike the flat tax. He advocates getting rid of the IRS (which everyone hates) and getting rid of the income tax. Instead, we would just have a great big national sales tax that would be collected on everything bought. Well, that has practically the same effect as the flat tax. It means that the people at the top end of the income scale are going to see their tax burdens drop precipitously and the people in the middle and bottom are going to see their tax burdens increase precipitously. I am therefore skeptical about whether that will sell either.

The only alternative left is what Congressman Kemp—who is presently sitting on a commission for the Republicans—wants to do, which is to redo the tax reform exercise of 1986. If some loopholes, tax breaks, and other things could be eliminated, the money saved could be used to bring down the rates while maintaining some progressivity in the rates to avoid a big change in the distribution of the tax burden. That approach might sell, but I do not think the more radical and the more superficially appealing plans have political "legs."

Regarding the states, yes, they are going to get hit hard here. The federal government is buying off the states by saying "no strings attached," but there is not much money that the strings are not going to be attached to, and the states will feel the squeeze.

Whether they choose to absorb that decrease in funds or raise taxes will vary from state to state.

QUESTION: Assuming that the recently announced Republican House program, the Senate program, or something along those lines becomes enacted, many people will be hurt. As a consequence, the people's support for the freshmen and sophomore members of Congress will be tested. Will they be thrown out of office after the country begins feeling the pain, and then will we go through the whole process again?

MR. MURRAY: It is hard to believe that support for deficit reduction will last through 2002. The question is, when does the opposition begin to occur? Is it next week, next month, or next year? Does it kick in three years from now? The polls indicate an unbelievable level of public support for reducing the deficit right now. Everyone wants to reduce government spending. If specific categories of spending are broken down, approximately 70 percent of the American people want to spend less on welfare, but strictly speaking, that is only a small part of the budget, if Medicaid is not included. Then they want to spend less on foreign aid, but that is only one percent of the budget. Likewise, everyone wants to spend less on the arts and the humanities, which does not even show up in percentage charts on the budget. Opinions toward those three budget items are pretty clear. Interestingly, however, even though some people would say that nutrition programs are part of welfare, 65 to 70 percent of the people responding to our polls say we should spend *more* money on government nutrition programs. Likewise, 70 percent want to spend more money on education programs. The most interesting part is that a large majority, 60 to 70 percent, say they want to spend more money on senior citizens, and the percent is even higher among people 20 to 35 years old than among the senior citizens. A great deal of public support for much of this government spending is about to get whacked. Either people's opinions are going to have to change, or at some point between now and 2002, there is going to be a revolt.

NARRATOR: I hope Alan Murray will have a long, Walter Lippmannesque career in journalism and continue to write until he is 90 years old. Your presentation was a *tour de force*, and we are all very grateful.

« CHAPTER 2 »

THE BUDGET DEFICIT AND THE NATIONAL DEBT: A BUDGET DIRECTOR'S CONSERVATIVE VIEW*

JAMES C. MILLER III

NARRATOR: James C. Miller III is currently counselor to Citizens for a Sound Economy and co-chairman of the Tax Foundation. He is also a John M. Olin Distinguished Fellow at the Citizens for a Sound Economy Foundation and the Center for Study of Public Choice at George Mason University, a senior fellow (by courtesy) of the Hoover Institution at Stanford University, and a member of the board of the Progress and Freedom Foundation.

Mr. Miller was director of the Office of Management and Budget (OMB) and a member of President Reagan's Cabinet from October 1985 to October 1988. From October 1981 to October 1985, he was chairman of the Federal Trade Commission. He was an associate director of OMB from January 1981 to October 1981, at which time he was responsible for the establishment of President Reagan's program of regulatory relief.

James Miller received a doctorate in economics from the University of Virginia in 1969. He has written and published over 100 articles in professional journals and has contributed to the *Wall*

Presented in a Forum at the Miller Center of Public Affairs on 23 May 1995.

Street Journal, the *Washington Post*, and the *New York Times*. He is the author, co-author, or editor of eight books, the most recent of which is *Fix the U.S. Budget: Urgings of an "Abominable No-Man"* published by the Hoover Institution. In addition, he often is asked to comment on public issues on such television programs as the "Today Show," "CBS Morning News," "Good Morning America," "MacNeil-Lehrer NewsHour," "Crossfire," and other news programs.

During the 1994 Virginia Republican party convention, Mr. Miller received 45 percent of the unit votes and over 50 percent of the delegate votes for nomination as candidate for the U.S. Senate. [Narrator's editorial note: In July 1996, he lost the Republican nomination to incumbent John Warner.]

Mr. Miller's background qualifies him to discuss the budget deficit and the national debt, and we welcome his comments.

MR. MILLER: I would like to begin by putting the budget issue in a broader context relating to other issues. There are two matters of great concern. One is language. The United States has a rather government-centric language when public policy issues are discussed, especially at the national level. As a result, people look naturally to the public sector to solve problems rather than to the private sector. Thus, if government is to be downsized, as many people favor, the way language is used to describe public policy must be changed.

A classic example is use of the word *fair*, as in "fair deals," "fair housing," and "fair taxes." Anyone opposing such proposals must be in favor of "unfair deals," "unfair housing," or "unfair taxes." The word *fair* is used quite often in names of bills brought before Congress because a bill is more likely to have co-sponsors and to obtain favorable hearings if the label *fair* is used. Another example of emotive language is the word "antidiscrimination." Anyone who opposes an antidiscrimination proposal must be in favor of discrimination. Likewise, if an antitrust proposal is submitted, the people who oppose it—maybe for good reasons—are held guilty of being in favor of big trusts and big monopolies.

Not only is there labeling, there is relabeling. When President Reagan introduced a proposal for the Strategic Defense Initiative (SDI), the opponents nicknamed it "Star Wars" and tried to make it a joke. The recent proposal by the House of Representatives to convert the school lunch program into a block grant to the states and actually increase total funding by 4 percent conjured up the rallying cry, "Catsup is a vegetable"—the contemporary analogue to "Let them eat cake!"

I was involved in the original catsup-is-a-vegetable episode. When I was the regulatory "czar" at OMB at the beginning of the Reagan administration, I sent a notice to regulatory officials at all of the agencies, saying that before they promulgated any major regulation, they had to send the draft regulation to me ten days in advance so that I could examine it and let the appropriate people know about it. The so-called catsup-is-a-vegetable rule arrived on my desk the same day it appeared in the *Federal Register*, thus arriving ten days late.

The main purpose of the proposed rule was to maximize the amount of protein in school lunch programs throughout the country. Meal planners were urged to "mix and match" from various categories. Catsup was listed under the vegetable category. Most people know that catsup is made from tomatoes and thus has a similar protein content as tomatoes and other tomato products.

The next day, "catsup is a vegetable" was a front-page story in most newspapers. At approximately 11:00 a.m., I was asked to go to David Stockman's office. He told me that something needed to be done about the catsup-is-a-vegetable rule, that the rule needed to be recalled. I replied that although I had not received the rule on time and had chastised the folks at Agriculture for their oversight, I thought the rule made sense in that its purpose was to maximize protein for children in the school lunch program. After the lunch hour, however, I received a note from Stockman, asking me to come to see him again. He told me that I had to "pull" the catsup-is-a-vegetable rule because the President just told a group of editors in the Oval Office he was having it pulled. He then told me to call Secretary of Agriculture Jack Block and relay the President's order to him. I did so, and a really good regulation was shot down because of language.

Language is a major problem when discussing the budget. For instance, tax cuts are often characterized by those in the media as "costs." To whom is a tax cut a cost? It is a cost to the government, but it is not a cost to the taxpayer. It seems to me a basic premise for our country and our society is that the person stands first and the government second. I would not characterize a tax cut as a cost. But such a characterization makes it more difficult for the cuts to be enacted.

One of the most vexing language problems with the budget is the "current services" concept. When families have financial crises and they talk about spending cuts, they mean that they will attempt to spend less next month than they have during the current month or less the next year than during the current year. That is *not* the way such language is used in Washington, however. When politicians talk about cutting spending, they mean to spend less next year than would have been spent if the budget were left on automatic pilot; that is, a spending "cut" is a reduction in the rate of increase in spending, not a reduction in the level of spending. (The same kind of language trick is used with respect to the revenue side.)

This method of defining "cuts" has a very pernicious effect. Various people in the media have reported numerous times that the Republican House and Senate are incorporating terrible *cuts* in their budget resolutions. Slash and burn! Yet, both houses of Congress envision increased spending, not a reduction in spending. The rate of growth in spending is lowered, but total spending goes up, not down.

It might surprise people to learn that the budget could be balanced without great difficulty if spending were simply "frozen"— not allowed to increase for a few years. A recent study by the Congressional Budget Office showed that if Congress froze nominal spending, the deficit would be eliminated by fiscal year 1998. A growing economy creates additional tax revenue every year, so the federal government usually receives some $70 billion or $80 billion more each year. If a recession occurred, it would take longer to reduce the deficit, but if the economy really boomed, the deficit could be eliminated earlier.

Many people say that such a strategy is not reasonable because "everyone knows" that a politician is crazy if he or she proposes to reduce spending for Social Security, and "everyone knows" that Social Security spending has to rise. Actually, the total level of spending can be frozen and there would still be additional money for Social Security increases. Every program would not have to be frozen. Some could be increased and some decreased. But if the government froze total spending on everything else and allowed Social Security to increase, the budget could be balanced by fiscal year 1999. The same is true of the Medicare program. If spending were frozen on everything else and allowances were made for increased spending on Medicare, the budget could still be balanced by fiscal year 1999.

One other frequently heard argument is that the budget cannot be balanced if the tax cuts included in the House Contract with America were allowed. On the contrary, it could be done. If spending is frozen while allowing for the revenue shortfall caused by the tax cuts in the House budget resolution, the budget could still be balanced by fiscal year 1999. One question people may have is, what about combinations of these proposals?

One such combination would be to allow scheduled Social Security and Medicare increases to go forward. This approach would put off a budget balance until fiscal year 2001. When the House and the Senate were debating the balanced budget amendment, which required a balanced budget by the year 2002 or two years after ratification depending upon which option came later, many people asked how the budget could possibly be balanced that quickly. The answer, as I have just told you, is reasonably simple, and it could be achieved without making any changes in Medicare or Social Security.

The problem of excessive growth in Medicare and Social Security will have to be addressed at some point, of course, but again, both could be exempted from any spending freeze and also have the tax cuts in the Contract and still balance the budget by fiscal year 2002. It just takes a commitment not to increase total spending on other programs.

Back to my point about language. With respect to budgeting, there is a tremendous gulf between reality and what people are led to believe about the situation. Bad decisions can occur when this kind of gulf between fact and perception exists, and steps should be taken to improve people's perceptions and thus lead to better decisions.

In making a major change in public policy, it is extremely important to reach a broad consensus over principles. During the Civil War, President Lincoln got a broad consensus, at least in the North, on preserving the Union and opposing slavery. Only then was he able to move forward and have the people of the North incur the enormous costs needed for victory. Franklin Roosevelt was able to implement the New Deal in the same way. President Reagan convinced people that the government was too large, too intrusive, too prone to regulate, and too inefficient. Having reached consensus on those principles, policy changes naturally followed.

The election of 1994 also affirms a consensus that government is too large and too intrusive and that something needs to be done. Furthermore, there is broad agreement that deficit finance is a bad idea. If the government is to operate, it must have command over resources. There are four principal ways the federal government can do this. Taxing and spending is the usual way. Borrowing and spending is another. A third way is for the federal government, which holds a monopoly on the medium of exchange, simply to print more money and spend it. The implicit "tax" of inflation is reflected in the eroding real value of the cash balances people hold. Finally, conscription can be used as a means of achieving command over resources. Although people do not usually think of our national government using conscription, a great deal of what people call regulation is in effect conscription because the government decrees where real resources are to be allocated.

The public is increasingly critical of deficit financing. Exit polls show there is a broad consensus that the government is too large or too imposing and that the deficit, which helps support this largesse, must be eliminated. As far as just *how* to cut the size of government and to eliminate the deficit, there is no particular consensus. Accordingly, I think a key to bringing about programmatic changes is first to get people to agree on basic principles. Let me suggest four of these principles.

First, government programs should be carefully scrutinized and decisions should be made concerning which of them are appropriately government functions and which are not. Those which are not true government functions should be spun off to the private sector. For example, I do not believe the federal government should run a passenger rail system. Amtrak should be privatized just as the government's freight railroad, Conrail, was. The weather service of the Department of Commerce should be privatized. Why shouldn't it compete on a more level playing field with Accuweather? The Postal Service should be demonopolized and privatized. Though mentioned and authorized in the U.S. Constitution, a government postal service is not mandated.

Second, we should ask which of the remaining programs should be federal functions and which more appropriately should be state and local functions. Such judgements should be made on both the practical merits of who could do the best job and by reading what the Constitution does and does not authorize for the federal government. On those grounds, education responsibilities, except for research, would be taken away from the federal government and given back to the states. Most medical programs, such as Medicare and Medicaid, should be state responsibilities. States could administer these programs through voucher systems. Making use of states as laboratories for policy experimentation is important. Moreover, many of the welfare programs would be better administered by the states and, in fact, by the private sector.

Third, a decision should be made as to which of the remaining government programs are either inefficient or clearly causing harm. Some programs might have once had good intentions but are now beyond redemption. On those grounds, the National Endowment for the Arts (NEA) and the National Endowment for the Humanities (NEH) are beyond the pale and should be eliminated. The NEH put together a standard for teaching history that does not even mention the U.S. Constitution, Orville and Wilbur Wright, or Robert E. Lee. The NEA subsidizes many activities that most people will find redeeming, such as symphony presentations. Unfortunately, it also subsidizes some things that most Americans find despicable, and that is simply wrong.

One candidate for elimination of particular interest to me is the Interstate Commerce Commission (ICC). When I presented my first budget to President Reagan, I said that if there ever was a public interest rationale for the ICC, it was long gone. I believed that the commission created harm by limiting competition and causing inefficiency in surface transportation and thus should be closed down. President Reagan agreed. That incident is one of the highlights of my experience in government. Academics have written about the defects of the ICC for 50 years, and nothing has happened. Our attempts to close it were not successful, but I think this year the ICC will go the way of the Civil Aeronautics Board, which was closed in 1985.

Finally, the remaining programs should be examined to determine which ones could be improved. What techniques and incentives used in the private sector could help a government program become more efficient? For example, what about incentive pay for rank-and-file employees of the federal government, members of Congress, and also for the president? In the private sector, incentives are widely used, especially for senior managers. If they perform well, they get a bonus; if they perform poorly, they do not get a bonus, and some even get a pay cut or are fired. This approach could be used in the public sector as well.

Productivity standards need to be established and agencies encouraged to meet them. In the private sector, if productivity is not increased every year, a company could go out of business. In the public sector, if an agency does not increase productivity, it gets *more* money because people think it did not have enough resources to begin with. Talk about perverse incentives! President Reagan signed an executive order establishing productivity standards for agencies, but the follow-up over the years has not exploited fully the opportunities for productivity improvement.

QUESTION: All of these budget plans extend to six or seven years in the future, but there is an implicit or perhaps explicit assumption about how the economy will perform in the second, third, fourth, or fifth year. Is that wise?

MR. MILLER: These plans are not based on arbitrary assumptions; they follow logic. If a program is changed in a certain way, the expenditures for each of the "out years" will be lower than they would have been, producing what is called a "wedge" effect. In some cases the plans postpone enactment of a policy change until the next year. For example, sometimes there are tax increases in the budget reconciliation bill that do not take effect in the first year but show up in subsequent years. I was once in the Oval Office when Dan Rostenkowski and others from Capitol Hill assured President Reagan that there were no tax increases in their reconciliation bill. Of course, there *were* tax increases for the out years. It is rather like a computer virus: It just suddenly shows up, and a tax hike is included that people did not know about but now have to pay.

Nevertheless, your point is well taken. Most of the diminution in the deficit is due to changes in the programs that would be initiated this year, specifically by cutting the generosity of the benefits of entitlement programs and by tightening eligibility requirements. That strategy naturally has a bigger effect in the out years.

QUESTION: Do there have to be seven annual concurrent budget resolutions?

MR. MILLER: Yes; Congress is not making a firm commitment to seven years. For example, when I submitted my first budget for fiscal year 1987, we had intended to achieve a balanced budget by 1991, in line with Gramm-Rudman-Hollings. I was hopeful that Congress would commit to all of the changes I had recommended, but they only committed to some of them. Consequently, the deficit was reduced from $221 billion to $150 billion, a record $71 billion in one year, but it did not stay down. In fact, it went back up to $155 billion the next year.

When President Clinton, Leon Panetta, and Alice Rivlin talk about reducing the deficit to a "historical low," they are talking about matching the record set in fiscal year 1987. Although this was quite an achievement, I was not satisfied, and during the 1987 budget summit negotiations, I almost resigned over the question of a tax increase, which I opposed. President Reagan was then embroiled in the Iran-contra controversy, and he did not have the political capital to insist that the deficit reductions be continued solely through restraints on spending. We did manage, however, to prevent any big increases in taxes or spending—which, in retrospect, appears to have been a great achievement.

On a related point, let me observe that whereas the current Senate plan merely cuts back on spending increases for many agencies, the House plan kills agencies altogether. I have had enough experience in government to know that if Congress and the administration think an agency is really awful—beyond redemption—and merely cuts its spending, the agency will simply come back at some point. That is why, on this account, the House plan is much better.

Let me comment briefly on the tax elements in the Contract with America. By far the biggest item—in terms of "lost revenue" to the government and direct benefits to taxpayers—is the $500 per dependent tax credit. A similar element, but one that would yield substantial long-run benefits, is cutting the capital gains tax rate in half and indexing the capital base for inflation. Many people pay a tax on phony gains because of inflation. The expanded IRAs are also important to economic growth. For the most part, however, the tax package contained in the Contract with America is not designed for economic purposes per se, but for basic fairness and good sense.

Another issue addressed by the Contract is the marriage penalty tax. Under certain circumstances with today's tax code, two people can be living together and pay less in federal taxes than if they were married filing a joint return. This situation is insane! Families are important institutions, but under the current tax law people are penalized for forming a family.

Since both the House and Senate budget proposals would balance the budget by the year 2000, it is clear that spending over the period in the House package is lower than in the Senate package because the House package has to make up for the loss of revenue in the Contract with America.

Next year there will be a big debate over a broad range of tax proposals. Bill Archer wants a consumption tax, but some version of Dick Armey's flat tax is more likely to be passed and signed into law by 1997. In my more partisan moments, I joke that President Clinton's tax plan has just two lines: (1) How much did you make last year? and (2) Send it in. The flat-tax plan is not that simple, but it is similar, though not as confiscatory. How much a person earned is put on line one and their allowance is put on line two. If the individuals are married, filing jointly, the proposed allowance is $26,200. (These numbers may be changed.) The amount is $13,100 for a single person and $17,200 for a single person who is the head of a household. Then an allowance of $5,300 is added for each dependent. After the allowances are totaled, that amount is subtracted from what the tax filer earned and the remainder is taxed at a flat rate of 17 percent, regardless of income level. It is a simple tax plan. There are no deductions, just allowances for the taxpayer(s) and dependents.

Keep in mind that up to a certain income level, zero tax is paid, and then tax is paid at a constant rate. Obviously, one could either change the point where payment of tax begins or change the slope of the line (i.e., the tax rate). Those are the trade-offs, and the combinations will be much debated. For instance, should the personal allowance for a married couple be $20,000, $26,000, or maybe $30,000?

Many people argue that the flat tax is regressive, which is false. The conventional definition of a regressive income tax is that the proportion of gross income paid in taxes decreases as income increases. That is *not* true of the flat tax. The average tax rate steadily rises as income rises, and the marginal tax rate is above the average tax rate. Thus, the proportion of reportable income that a person pays in taxes is always greater at higher levels of income. The flat tax is, in fact, *progressive*.

The proposed flat tax is very similar to the first U.S. income tax in 1913. The whole packet had only four pages—one page for figuring the tax, the second page for totaling income, the third page for totaling deductions, and the last page containing the instructions for completing the form. After subtracting exemptions, the amount of tax owed was 1 percent of the amount over $20,000 but not exceeding $50,000. The top tax rate for income over $500,000 was only 6 percent. We have come a long way from 1913 to today, with Dick Armey's proposed flat tax rate of 17 percent.

QUESTION: How does the flat tax concept handle tax-free investments?

MR. MILLER: Investments would no longer be tax free.

COMMENT: Having no tax-free investments would ruin the market for municipal bonds. I do not think the financial structure could handle that situation.

MR. MILLER: I think it could. The flat tax will have three major points of criticism. One, the mortgage deduction would be eliminated. Many people would be worried about that, but there is a trade-off: People would get lower marginal tax rates and a zero rate for a large part of their income. Many people today do not use all of their mortgage deduction because the amount of interest that can be deducted is limited. In addition, there would be lower interest rates (how much lower is uncertain), so there would be lower mortgage payments on this account.

The second point of contention will be the elimination of deductions for charitable contributions. With a lower marginal tax rate, the gain from giving to charity will be lower as well—but believe it or not, historically, charitable contributions show little response to changes in marginal tax rates. Giving is highly related to national income, and a flat tax will stimulate growth. People making donations tend to be motivated by charity rather than some kind of tax write-off.

The third controversy will be over municipal bonds. Cities will simply have to compete for capital in the open market like everyone else. They will not have a preferentially lower rate of interest. Surely municipalities can float bond issues without the special tax advantages offered today. They may pay somewhat more and it may be a little more difficult, but it is not as though they would no longer be able to borrow money.

COMMENT: They would just have to pay a premium.

MR. MILLER: No, they would be like everyone else. They would pay more than they pay now, but they would pay like everyone else. A fundamental premise of the flat tax is that everyone is treated equally.

Citizens for Sound Economy conducted some focus groups in which people were asked about their attitudes toward taxes. These focus groups revealed that people are very concerned about horizontal equity. To put it in the vernacular, those who are paying all of their taxes suspect that their neighbors are somehow managing to get by without paying all of the tax they owe. They figure that a flat tax would be harder for their neighbors to evade. Also, they like the idea of tax simplicity. These two big attractions of the flat tax do not have much to do with economics as narrowly defined.

QUESTION: How confident do you feel that the projected downward trend in deficits would actually continue in light of the debate currently going on in Washington?

MR. MILLER: If Congress had passed the balanced budget amendment, then I would feel very confident, but it did not pass—although it may pass next year. Bob Dole did the trick of voting against his own proposal so he would have a chance to bring it up again. When the heat of public pressure is brought to bear, the amendment may pass. Though many people are upset with the 5-to-4 decision of the Supreme Court on term limits, term limits will not have the appeal that one might expect because much of the pent-up anger behind public support for term limits has been dissipated with the big turnover of people in Congress. I would feel much better if a balanced budget amendment to the Constitution had been ratified. Getting it out of Congress is one hurdle; getting it ratified by 34 states is something else.

When I wrote President Reagan's 1987 budget, I was convinced that his administration would succeed in controlling spending because I thought there was a wellspring of enthusiasm in the country to eliminate the deficit. The plan was a good one, an institutional arrangement whereby the "robot" came out and clobbered people if the deficit was not reduced. Unfortunately, there was a strong feeling in Congress that spending restraints were too tight, even though nominal spending went up every year under my plan. The stock market collapse in October 1987 provided the excuse for Congress to demand that President Reagan agree to the reframing of the provisions of Gramm-Rudman-Hollings. It is rather interesting that some of the leaders of Congress came to the President and said that the market collapsed because the deficit was too high. Their solution was to revise Gramm-Rudman-Hollings so as to raise the deficit even more. It reminds me of the last State of the Union address that President Reagan gave when he held up the enormous stack of papers comprising the Budget Reconciliation Act. He said, "You send me another one of these and I will not sign it." Ironically, he got a standing ovation from the very people who had sent the mess to him in the first place!

QUESTION: Assuming that balancing the budget is of transcendent importance, do you see any nonpolitical justification for coupling initiatives in that direction with tax reform? Aren't these problems completely unrelated?

MR. MILLER: No, I do not think they are unrelated problems. Cutting taxes certainly can yield revenue shortfalls that would make it more difficult to balance the budget if everything else were equal. If the government gets too caught up in balancing the budget, however, it might make some bad decisions. For example, if public enthusiasm for balancing the budget rises sharply but the dominant legislative coalition opposes any restraint on spending, there will probably be higher tax rates so that revenue will be raised. That measure, however, simply tends to reinforce the existing propensity for spending to increase.

A few years ago I conducted an econometric test in which I took the last 25 years of data and asked the question, which is more effective in reducing the deficit—restraints on spending or increases in tax rates? Not surprisingly, I found that restraints on spending had a definite effect on the deficit, but that increasing tax rates had virtually no effect. There are two hypotheses to explain that finding. One is that the country is at what Jude Wanniski calls the "bliss point" on the Laffer curve. The other is a behavioral function of Congress whereby if Congress is given more money, it will spend it. I think the latter is probably the better explanation.

The country should have lower tax rates, but I have never believed in the simpleminded version of the Laffer curve. The official papers of the Reagan administration show that the administration never argued that lowering tax rates would generate more revenue immediately. It did say that lowering tax rates in certain circumstances would increase economic activity and that the reduction in tax revenue would be less than the result obtained from multiplying the tax rate change by the existing revenue base. We in the administration never painted a simple Santa Claus scenario in which cutting tax rates is supposed to be good for conservatives because they pay lower taxes and are also good for liberals because they have more money to spend.

QUESTION: If investors are holding a municipal bond at 6 percent and the average going rate is 8 percent, the tax deductibility is lost, and those investors are probably going to lose a great deal of principal value. On a different subject, could you define what entitlement programs are?

MR. MILLER: Current holders of municipal bonds would probably be protected by a grandfather clause.

So-called entitlement programs are programs whose budgets will automatically be increased even if there is no change in law. President Reagan used to say, "I cannot spend a dime that Congress doesn't appropriate." That is not quite true, Mr. President! Social Security, Medicare, Medicaid, the farm program, the student loan program, and many other entitlement programs do indeed go forward even if there is an absolute deadlock between the White House and Congress. Congress does not have to do a thing. When I was budget director, Congress's irresponsible refusal to deal with the administration used to befuddle me. Congress is supposed to pass all of the appropriation bills by 1 October, when the fiscal year begins. The president then must sign these bills so that the Defense Department, the Justice Department, and other agencies can continue operating. Congress would wait until the last minute, however, and there would be a big tussle because Congress would insist on a tax increase and I would say no on behalf of the President. At the end of the year, everything would be rolled into a "continuing resolution," which was basically a law that continued the existing rate of appropriations. (They would always put little extra goodies in here and there.) It would have a cutoff date, and after that date, if no agreement were reached, everything was supposed to stop and all of the government workers would be sent home. I remember on one such occasion being in the Oval Office with the President, walking up and down the carpet, upset about why Congress acted so irresponsibly. The President told me: "Jim, Jim, just settle down. Let's close her down and see if anyone notices!"

QUESTION: Under the flat tax, would any forms of income be nontaxable?

MR. MILLER: No taxes would be paid on corporate stock dividends because the tax would already have been paid. Retirement benefits from funds already taxed would not be taxed again, but certain insurance proceeds would be taxed—that portion would be viewed as an investment. All of those specific questions are still pending final determination.

QUESTION: Would the flat tax also apply to corporations?

MR. MILLER: Yes, there would be a corporate income tax rate handled in much the same way. Basically, human resource expenses, supplies, materials, and other expenses would be totaled and subtracted from total revenue, and a flat tax would be paid on the remainder. It would be handled just as the personal income tax would be, and the same flat tax rate percentage would apply. That is the Dick Armey plan.

Senator Arlen Specter has proposed a different flat tax plan. His plan allows some deductions for mortgage interest and charitable contributions. He does not do anything on municipal bonds, however, which is the third point of contention I mentioned.

I oppose the so-called consumption tax on practical grounds. In theory, it makes some sense because the present tax code tends to tax savings and investment too much, in effect subsidizing consumption. A consumption tax is a better idea because a great deal of economic growth would be generated by having more savings and investment. Unfortunately, when a plan is proposed to Congress that it substitute one tax for another, usually the country gets both taxes, and I am really concerned about that prospect. One possibility would be to pass a consumption tax that is effective upon ratification of a constitutional amendment that eliminates the 16th Amendment, which allows for the income tax. That way, the plan would be sure to work.

QUESTION: Would capital expenditures of corporations be treated as expenses?

MR. MILLER: Yes, they will be expensed—not subject to depreciation.

QUESTION: What inflation rate is implied in the future?

MR. MILLER: Although I do not have the assumptions with me, a reasonable projection of future inflation rates is about 3 or 4 percent annually. Because the Federal Reserve has been much too stringent on the monetary aggregates, economic growth will not be as robust this coming year as the administration has forecast.

NARRATOR: We are grateful to Mr. Miller for his discussion of the budget deficit and for explaining the current proposed tax plans.

CHAPTER 3

THE BUDGET DEFICIT AND ITS IMPACT ON CITIES*

JERRY E. ABRAMSON

NARRATOR: Jerry Abramson was first elected mayor of Louisville in 1985 with a record 73 percent of the vote. He has since been reelected twice, the first time an individual has been elected to a third four-year term in over a century in Louisville. He has improved the city services and implemented citizen-access programs called "Mayor's Night In" and "Mayor's Night Out."

Mr. Abramson has been uniquely successful in encouraging public-private partnership in the areas of affordable housing, the environment, teenage pregnancy, and children in poverty. For those efforts, the National Association of Home Builders named him Local Public Official of 1994, and in 1993 the U.S. Conference of Mayors gave him the Michael A. diNunzio Special Award. He also launched Operation Brightside, an environmental cleanup and beautification program under which over 700,000 flowers were planted and more than 100,000 tons of trash were collected.

Mr. Abramson has been involved in recycling programs and has headed an effort to develop and improve the Louisville airport. He has revitalized the downtown waterfront, thus gaining for Louisville

---

Presented in a Forum at the Miller Center of Public Affairs on 13 June 1995.

the designation of "Enterprise Community" and securing for Louisville $3 million in federal funds to provide more job training programs and job transportation and to encourage business in his city's impoverished neighborhoods. He is one of the most visible municipal officials in the United States. He will speak on the budget deficit problem and its impact on the cities.

MR. ABRAMSON: When I was asked to deliver this lecture, I felt like the token heretic being invited to a meeting of the Inquisition. Keep in mind that heretics are often valuable for questioning dogma and notions that are taken on faith, which is what I am here to discuss today.

In my opinion, the Contract with America that is behind the current congressional move to balance the budget is based more on an unquestioning acceptance of some very questionable assumptions rather than on logic, history, or truth. The Newt Gingrich Republicans and the right-wing Rush Limbaugh-style of radio programs have had tremendous success in winning the hearts and minds of the American people to their point of view. They generally argue that liberalism is bad, while conservatism is good; taxes are too high; the federal government is too intrusive; the federal government cannot do anything right and its programs should be ended or turned over entirely to the states. That article of faith is preached day after day in the rhetoric on the radio and in the halls of Congress, but their assumptions are questionable and historically inaccurate.

The federal government has been a catalyst for progress and the spreading of prosperity to a wider segment of the population than in any other country in the world. Examples of the federal government's key role in this country's development begins with the day when Thomas Jefferson signed the Louisiana Purchase in 1803 and continues through the Homestead Act of 1862 that settled the western states, the land grant college era beginning in 1862 with the Morrill Act that made America's farmers and agricultural sector the best in the world, and Teddy Roosevelt's founding of the National Park System to conserve this country's natural beauty. Other examples include the post–World War II GI Bill, which brought a widely educated populace; the Veterans Administration home loan program, which allowed widespread home ownership and thus the great prosperity of the 1950s; the Eisenhower interstate highway system; John Kennedy's space exploration program; Social Security, Medicare, Pell Grants, and more recently, the Head Start program; and science research programs. To deny the good that the federal initiatives have accomplished is in my judgment to deny the very history of the United States. To demonize each and every action of the federal government is to abrogate the ability to invest in infrastructure, technology, natural resources, and human capital in order to go forward as a nation.

Does the United States need to get its deficit spending under control? Does it need to make mid-course corrections and rid this country of outmoded programs that have outlived their usefulness? Does the bureaucracy that has overregulated in many areas need to be reined in? The answer to all of these questions, of course, is yes. But does the baby need to be thrown out with the bath water by having the federal government end all environmental regulations, slashing and burning federal investments in the future of the United States, and transferring all responsibility for human needs to the states? Doing so in my opinion would be a big mistake.

People need to be reminded that there was a reason in U.S. history that governmental power flowed away from the separate states toward the federal government. In my judgment the reason was because the United States had 50 states with 50 different sets of rules and regulations, and benefits were unwieldy, unmanageable, and ultimately unfair to certain citizens, depending on where they happened to live. It was the federal initiatives that ended racial segregation in the Southern states. It was the federal initiatives that leveled the playing field in important areas such as education that allowed poorer states to stay on par with the richer states. Before American citizens plunge into downsizing the federal government to pint-size proportions and devolving all power back to the states, perhaps this nation's history needs to be accurately recalled. Then the people can look truthfully at the federal government and what the Republican version of a balanced budget does *to* the people—not for the people—as a nation.

Lawyers always advise people to read the small print of any contract before signing it. The American people have not even

47

begun to read the large print in the Contract with America, much less understand the implications of the budget-balancing actions now being proposed in Washington. A recent story in the *New York Times* told of interviews conducted with "average" citizens in a middle-class community located in California in which they were asked, "What is the Contract with America?" Several people confused the Contract with the recent GATT trade agreement. One person thought it was a treaty with Mexico, and others simply were not sure what it contained. If most Americans were not sure what the Contract was, that ignorance is nothing compared to their lack of knowledge about how the federal government spends their tax money or what changes will be required to balance the budget.

Last Wednesday an article in the *New York Times* reported results of interviews conducted with retirees in Florida who were convinced beyond a doubt that the federal government spends more money on foreign aid than Medicare. The truth is, the government spends about $11 billion on foreign aid and $144 billion on Medicare. Many people thought more was spent on welfare in the United States than on Social Security. The fact is that about $17 billion was spent on Aid to Families with Dependent Children (AFDC) welfare and $319 billion was spent on Social Security in 1994. These widely held misconceptions cripple the U.S. government's ability to deal with the real budget problems—namely, entitlements—and the implications of their automatic growth. Few people know that over 70 percent of the current U.S. $1.6 trillion federal budget will be spent on just three categories: defense, interest on the debt, and benefits for the elderly. Few Americans know that two-thirds of the $90 billion Medicaid health care program created for the poor actually goes to maintain the elderly in nursing homes. Few take notice of the fact that the overwhelming majority of the $37 billion in the federal Veteran's budget is spent to maintain the elderly. When the budgets of Social Security, Medicare, and Medicaid are added together, the $619 billion of the $1.6 trillion overall budget goes to senior citizens—a figure that is 38 percent of the federal budget! If income security programs such as federal employee pensions, unemployment insurance, disability, Social Security supplemental benefits for the blind and disabled are included, fully 84 percent of the federal budget is spent on entitlements, defense, and interest on the debt. Thus, only 16 percent of the federal budget is available to fund a long list of vital programs: housing, roads, bridges, airports, scientific research, education, agriculture, natural resources, parks, energy, NASA, job training, health research, the environment, crime, and others. All of those programs' budgets amount to only 16 percent of the federal budget.

The Republicans want to balance the budget by slashing the 16 percent and then holding down increases in Medicare and other entitlements. By the year 2002, when the United States is supposed to reach a balanced budget at approximately $1.8 trillion, a whopping 93 percent of the budget will be spent on defense, interest on the debt, and entitlements, with 50 percent of the budget being spent on the elderly. Only 7 percent of the budget would be left for all of the other programs.

This forecast makes little sense in positioning the United States for the future. If the CEO of a major corporation told the board of directors that 93 percent of the corporation's budget would be spent on debt service, retirees, disabled workers, and security and only 7 percent on manufacturing, production development, sales, marketing, research and development, employee training, advertising, and distribution, that CEO would be fired for his negligence in not planning for the future. Similarly, the current budget proposals being made in Washington by the new majority party in Congress literally disinvests in the future of this nation. If the United States is to compete in a global economy, and I believe it has no choice, then failing to invest tax dollars in the people, the children, education, infrastructure, technology, science, and natural resources would be very shortsighted for this nation.

To cut $230 billion in domestic spending, which would include cuts of $21 billion in building and maintaining highways and airports, $67 billion in education and training programs, $1.4 billion in Head Start, and cuts in funds for foster care, child nutrition, and scientific research would be a disinvestment that would severely handicap the nation in competition in the global marketplace. If people strongly believe in a balanced budget, they should think carefully about whether this plan is the right way to accomplish it.

The Republicans should not be blamed entirely for the budget crisis; there is enough blame for all guilty parties. Members of the print and electronic media who are chasing each other down the low road of tabloid journalism deserve a share of the blame. When people in this country know more about O. J. Simpson's houseguests than they do about the spending priorities of the federal budget that so deeply affect each American, the media can take no bow. My own party—the Democratic party—uses the specter of so-called dire cuts of Medicare and Social Security to scare the wits out of the elderly whenever it is politically profitable to do so. Unfortunately, Democrats have thus seriously muddied the waters. No one is telling the truth to the American people—that this nation cannot continue to endlessly increase spending on entitlements without literally going bankrupt.

A rational debate needs to be held on how to control entitlements and balance the budget in such a way that the United States can take care of those people who truly need assistance and still ensure a bright future for this nation. That solution does not include leaving senior citizens homeless and facing poverty because of high medical bills or other difficulties. It does mean recognizing that men such as Lee Iacocca, Ross Perot, and Donald Trump do not need Social Security or Medicare. A means test could be used for some of those programs. This method would require explaining to the elderly that people who turn 65 this year on average will receive in seven years all of the money they have paid into Social Security plus interest and that they will receive four times as much in Medicare benefits over the rest of their lives as they have paid into that system. That reality is the basis for a rational discussion; those are the facts. It is also a fact that private pensions and health insurance are currently much more widespread and generous than when the original programs of the government safety net were created.

I readily admit that in today's atmosphere where law enforcement officers have been called jackbooted thugs wearing Nazi bucket helmets, it is very difficult to have rational debate. It is much easier to talk about the emotional issues of the moment and to argue over bumper-sticker slogans as if some simple solution could solve all of the problems. I must say, however, that as last year's president of the United States Conference of Mayors, we mayors are very frightened about what is occurring in the country today at the national level and the effect it will have on the quality of life in cities throughout the United States.

The reason for our fear is quite simple. Cities are at the bottom rung of the governmental "food chain." As everything devolves from the feds to the states to the counties to the cities, we have no one left to turn to. The cities are where the buck literally stops. As Congress begins to bundle programs into the new concept of block grants to cut funding levels by 30 and 40 percent and then to send them to the states to be divided among counties and cities, it is not good news for us mayors. State legislatures are too often controlled by rural and suburban areas and have little feel for urban problems. It is thus scant comfort when mayors are told that they will have so much more flexibility. In fact, the inadequate block grants will spark fights over whether the money should be spent on children or seniors programs. Should the money be spent on education or child care? The confrontation will occur at the state level where urban areas tend to play a very small role.

The Community Development Block Grant is the only grant that cities get directly from the federal government, but the Senate wants to cut that grant by 50 percent, and the House wants to cut it by 20 percent each year for the next seven years. These funds are used only for low-income housing, job training, child care, and so forth. That prospect does not make mayors optimistic about the future.

Likewise, the budget proposes to eliminate the summer-jobs-for-kids program. Eliminating that money would affect 1,000 children in Louisville, Kentucky, and 39,000 children in New York City. The person in my community most concerned about next summer is the police chief because thousands of children will be standing on corners with nothing to do but get into trouble. That news is especially not good when the Republicans propose cutting off welfare recipients completely after two years with no job training, no child care, no transportation to the workplace, and no support or assistance whatsoever. Ending welfare benefits immediately for pregnant teenagers and legal immigrants would impose an additional burden on mayors. It is not good news to mayors

51

when Republicans propose an end to federal rental assistance; Section 8 housing certificates are relied upon by 1,300,000 families who otherwise would have no place to live. It is not good news for mayors when Republicans propose an $8 billion cut in maintenance of public housing facilities. People can argue over whether public housing is being handled properly, but the point is that without public housing, many thousands of people would not have a place to live. Taking away the wherewithal to fix the toilets or ensuring that ceilings do not leak makes little sense.

We mayors have done a good job of finding innovative solutions to the problems we face. *Reinventing Government: How the Entrepreneurial Spirit is Transforming the Public Sector* (1992) by David Osborne and Ted Gaebler describes a wide variety of non-federal programs that displayed real innovation. Laboratories of change are occurring at the local level of cities and counties. Mayors are prepared to do their part, but it is not just a problem of the poor or the minorities in urban communities. Their plight will have a direct effect on everyone in this nation. Demographic projections show that a much greater percentage of nation's labor force in the future will be composed of African-Americans, Hispanics, Asian-Americans, and women. There is an inverted population pyramid in the United States. More and more people are growing older while fewer and fewer are having children. When I graduated from high school, the United States could afford in effect to disregard the bottom 25 percent of each high school class. Now every child needs to be fully prepared so that the economy of this nation will be strong and competitive in the future. The inner-city black child cannot be discarded; neither can the Hispanic children living in the barrio of San Antonio nor the eastern Kentucky white children living in Appalachia. The businesses of the future will need educated and skilled employees to ensure a positive future for the United States.

A perfect example is Kentucky, whose birthrate ranks 49th in the nation. Not a single person can be wasted. Every child needs to be a part of the future economic fabric of Kentucky's commonwealth so that the state can have the kind of economy and quality of life everyone wants. The United States thus faces a critical issue: If this country does not provide support for its children, student college loans are cut, school lunch programs are cut, public housing is closed down, and children are dodging bullets in their neighborhoods, what kind of country will the people have in terms of a competitive work force? How will the government ensure that the poor and legal immigrants have the same opportunities to improve their quality of life? The government cannot afford to leave them behind.

I spoke at the Homestead resort a couple of years ago to 150 CEOs of top corporations in America at the National Business Round Table. I told them that the crisis facing the cities would eventually affect the bottom line of all of their companies. When a CEO is grabbed by his or her bottom line, the heart and wallet soon follows. I tried to emphasize how important it was for them to care about the urban issues and how important it was to understand that children today will be the employees of tomorrow. As a result, four of the CEOs were persuaded to testify before Congress about the importance of fully funding Head Start and the Women, Infants, and Children (WIC) program.

In my judgment, the proposals by the Newt Gingrich organization in Washington are not only mean-spirited, but short-sighted as well. They play on the fears of the middle class and make scapegoats out of the least fortunate people in this society. If the clock were turned back and the United States had refused to educate immigrants and pushed people into poverty and homelessness, it would have destroyed the ability to create a competitive, high-skilled future work force. As Washington is convulsed with the budget-cutting fervor aimed at the poor and the immigrants, it is the cities that will have to bear the brunt, yet the cities can no longer cope with those problems. America's problems cannot be solved by feeding the politically powerful suburbs while starving the inner-cities. Nor can this country starve the transportation network that moves goods across state lines or starve airports, public transportation facilities, energy resources, or natural resources. It cannot afford to starve its great universities whose scientific, medical, economic, and social research feeds the discovery of new cures, new technology, and new paths to progress.

This is a very divisive time in our country. It is a time when Americans are focused on what divides them as a nation—race, gender, sexual orientation, ethnic background, age, and economic class. In short, many issues have been framed as "us against them," and it is popular in politics to play on these divisions. To approach the problem that way, however, is a losing game. Americans are at their best when they are called upon to undertake great endeavors for a higher purpose, whether it is pioneering new territory, fighting a world war, or putting a man on the moon. In such times, the real strength of the nation is proven. Unfortunately, the Contract with America and its method of balancing the budget would ultimately starve the American soul. It does not call the people to come together as a nation and invest in the promise of the future. Instead, it invites the people to break down further as a nation along economic, class, racial, and ethnic lines. In my judgment, it is not giving back to the states so much as it is abdicating a national purpose. In this country today there is an absence of hope for people coming together for the common good and working together to meet challenges. No investment in the people is being made.

The federal deficit is a serious problem, but it can be solved if people are truthful about its causes and try to work together to solve the problems. Restoring the national spirit, however, is a far deeper problem. Solving that problem will require vision and a new American dream. Until the people have that kind of vision, perhaps an old vision will suffice. Thomas Jefferson said in his inaugural speech in 1801:

> All, too, will bear in mind this sacred principle, that though the will of the majority is in all cases to prevail, that will to be rightful must be reasonable; that the minority possess their equal rights, which equal law must protect, and to violate would be oppression. Let us, then, fellow-citizens, unite with one heart and one mind. Let us restore to social intercourse the harmony and affection without which liberty and even life itself are dreary things.

I would submit that the Founding Fathers spoke the truth of their day and speak the truth of today as well. The American people should heed Thomas Jefferson's call to bring this country together and focus on the positive aspects of it as Americans debate the issue of what to do about the deficit.

QUESTION: Many people feel that what is being expressed by the Republican leadership today is not a mean-spirited attack seeking to deprive America's soul but a reflection of Jefferson's reasonable will of the people to restore working order to the country and a reflection of the fact that the welfare state has not achieved the expected results. Putting more money into the same old programs will not help reach that goal. How do you see these programs being redirected or reassessed in order to make them effective?

MR. ABRAMSON: Much innovation is occurring today in the public sector, as described by the book *Reinventing Government.* Cities have lost a significant amount of their financial base over the last 20 years, and they have had to do more with less. The real laboratories of innovation are the cities in the United States. I have told leaders of both parties as well as the President that much could be learned from how those people at the grass-roots level have been able to respond to the difficulties facing American communities. At the same time, however, cities need to have a partnership with the federal government because this country has evolved through cooperative orientation.

When the mind-set of this country is dominated by sloganeering and pretending that complex problems can be solved by several words on a bumper sticker, the rational debate is eroded. The perfect example is a child care program in a community in Louisville where 91 of the children's parents are either working or going through training. All of the parents of these children are living in public housing, and if the "slash and burn" approach to budget cutting continues, one day it will be all over for these people. Many of them are only making minimum wage, and without child care support, they would not have access to job training. If they lose the health care card for their children and access to transportation to get to work or to the community college, and if they lose their housing voucher, what will happen to those families and their children? These parents are doing it by the book. They are going back to school and back to the workplace, but their current level of education and skills only provides them with about $5 an hour. What will happen to these people? The emergency rooms of hospitals would become their primary health care facilities. That shift would have an affect on all other people's health insurance premiums. Where would they live? The shelters in communities are already full. Of course everyone wants to balance the budget. The old cliché that if I balance my checkbook every month, the government ought to do so isn't easy. It is a great slogan, but when people confront the ramifications of budget cutbacks, they see that these cuts produce complex problems. This country did not get into this fiscal predicament overnight, and it is not going to resolve it in five, six, or seven years.

My strong feeling about the deficit is that changes are needed. Far more administrative flexibility is needed, and programs need to be assessed to determine whether they are necessary. A full analysis of whether initiatives undertaken in the 1940s and 1950s are appropriate for the 1980s, 1990s, and the year 2000 needs to be made. These requirements are all legitimate. How can legal immigrants be told, however, that they will not receive government benefits as part of this nation? How does one say to a 15-year-old mother that as of tomorrow, she will not receive benefits? The slogans for balancing the budget sound great, but I am dealing with those problems every day. In the community center located in a public housing project, 72 percent of the residents are under the age of 15. Not one man lives in the whole place!

This country does need to make changes, but meanwhile, what will Americans do with the people in need of assistance, including the children and those who need job training? New York senator Daniel Patrick Moynihan's proposal would provide transitional health care, child care, and support for transportation to get to school or work, but it would cost the American people more in bottom line dollars than the programs being offered today do. I happen to favor that approach because although the costs are greater now, it will cost less in the long run.

Three out of five children living in the community in which I am mayor are below the poverty level. I have a son who is three-and-a-half years old, and when I take him to some of these public functions, I see children his age running around barefoot in the middle of the night and in diapers. It is not their fault that they are in this situation. My child will make it, but I am now beginning to understand why some mothers do the things they do to ensure that their children will make it. The American people have to begin to pull this society back together, or in a worse-case scenario, this country will have rioting in the streets. My colleagues across the country and I share this view. That is not to say that significant change is not occurring or that the welfare system does not includes some able-bodied people who should be working or that change is not wanted. I am a strong advocate of change, but nothing happens overnight, and nothing gets accomplished by a battle-cry slogan. Unfortunately, this country is lacking as a result of talk radio and gimmickry.

QUESTION: How do you propose to pay for these programs you are defending? They cannot be sustained indefinitely by borrowing funds.

MR. ABRAMSON: You are right. The programs can be paid for by prioritizing the budget, something I have to do every year. I submitted the budget last month to the Louisville city council, and the state of Kentucky requires cities to balance their budgets. All ten budgets during my tenure have had to be balanced. I received 150,000 requests, and I can only fund 110,000 of them. The others just don't get funded.

Human capital and investing in the people of the United States should be a top priority, whether it is the public universities or Head Start. Most all people make investments for the future. I am investing money now for my child's college education to invest in his future instead of buying something for myself right now. Likewise, this nation must adjust its budget priorities to ensure that its citizens have a strong nation in the future. That step can be taken by beginning to make some of the changes in entitlements.

My parents are not thrilled about my thinking on this subject, but when people see what is being spent on senior citizens versus what is being spent on children, it becomes obvious who votes in this country. Senator Alan Simpson from Wyoming is going to make that point this morning at hearings with the American Association of Retired Persons (AARP). They do many wonderful things, but it makes no sense to weaken the commitment to children year after year while maintaining a level of commitment to senior citizens that many would believe is far beyond what is necessary. When put in that perspective, people began to question how their tax dollars are prioritized.

QUESTION: What is your position on federal and state income taxes? Should tax rates go up or down?

MR. ABRAMSON: The *New York Times* recently published an article about how the percentage of the national work force employed by the federal government has decreased, while city and state government employment has in fact increased in relative terms. As people "devolve" many responsibilities down to the state and local level, it takes additional people to provide that support. Even if the government were to privatize half the programs that some people want privatized, public employees would still be needed to oversee the private contractors. I would thus suspect that if people follow that logic, taxes should decrease at the national level and increase at the local level. That situation, however, will not happen. Even though property taxes are extremely low in my community, no one wants to pay any more taxes.

In my opinion, if people are bombarded every day by negative comments on television, in newspapers, and especially on talk radio about how government is so horrendous and how people are paying too much in taxes, they begin questioning why they should pay these taxes because the government is just frittering it away. I admit that government officials make mistakes, but these critics never highlight the governmental successes in providing services to people at the local level.

I happen to be one of those peculiar people who appreciate what I receive for my tax dollars, and I do not resent having to pay my taxes on the 15th of April. I know that when I take my child to the parks there will be new play equipment, when I play golf at a public golf course there will be new tee boxes, and when I play tennis, the tennis courts will have been resurfaced. I am glad to pay for these services. Hardly anyone is glad to pay taxes, but I think paying taxes is part of being an American, and it is a fair price for the services people expect to receive from the government.

JERRY E. ABRAMSON

QUESTION: What prompted you to enter the public sphere?

MR. ABRAMSON: When I was president of the student body at Indiana University, Robert Kennedy entered the race for president, and Indiana was the first primary in which he ran. I was a big fan of his and traveled with him throughout the state. When I later went to Georgetown and worked actively on Capitol Hill, I made a decision that public service was where I wanted to be. I am a person who believes that the public sector has a role to play, and I like to be in the middle of all of the controversies going on in my community. I am a third-generation Louisvillian. After practicing law for many years and serving in the governor's cabinet in Frankfort for two years, I returned and continued to practice law. Having been on the city council for a couple of terms, I realized that what I really wanted to do was public service. Fortunately, I had been single for all of those years, so I had no family commitments and could thus afford to leave a lucrative law practice and run for mayor of Louisville in 1985, after which my salary was $48,000. Although I am happily married with a child and am basically going broke, I enjoy every minute of it.

QUESTION: I firmly agree with you on this need for rational discussion. How do you propose to promote that need?

MR. ABRAMSON: The problem is that politicians are very successful in the way the manipulate discourse in Washington. When I was president of the Conference of Mayors last year I brought a group of mayors to meet with Congressman Gingrich and his group of Republican leaders in the House (the Republicans were still the minority party in Congress at that time). We talked about the crime bill that the President had proposed under which 50 percent of the money would be spent on enforcement and about 50 percent on prevention. The mayors of this country were supportive of that idea, even Richard Riordan, the new Republican mayor of Los Angeles and Rudolph Giuliani, the Republican mayor of New York. The Republican opponents of the bill were talking about after-school activities—such as midnight basketball, which became a buzz word—as an example of "pork." We told Gingrich and all of these white Republicans how important crime prevention was. We also thought it was important to put more police on the streets for law enforcement. We were most concerned, however, about the five-, six-, and seven-year-old children of today who in ten years could become the criminals of tomorrow. Our police chiefs who came with us said that they would prefer giving funds and working with kids after school when they were seven years old than to fight these kids in the city alleys when they were 17 years old. Gingrich listened and then said that maybe they were wrong and maybe it was not pork after all. Unfortunately, after the meeting the cameras were blaring and the conversation returned to the same pork rhetoric. These big-city mayors do not understand the reality and that the days of throwing money at problems are gone. It wasn't just government programs we were discussing; many service providers are nonprofit organizations such as boys' and girls' clubs and YMCAs.

The point I am making with that example is that the cheap sound-bite tactics work. After the meeting with Gingrich, people in Louisville essentially said, "What do we need midnight basketball for? That's all pork. We need more cops!" One way or another, citizens have to see through the easy silver-bullet "solutions" and demand better of their elected officials.

I am not planning to run for any other political office after my term expires in three-and-a half more years. By then I will have served 13 years as mayor of the city of Louisville. At one time, however, I was considering the possibility of entering the senate race, and I asked Kentucky's incumbent senator what the pluses and minuses were of serving on Capitol Hill. He said there was no camaraderie and that the hatred was venomous. He said that it was a scorch earth policy—both sides would do whatever it took to make sure they won, including defaming their opponents. Then the senator said that nothing was ever accomplished. He said that he and his allies had fought the issue of assault weapons in the House and won and that they had fought it in the Senate and won. They then went to a conference committee and kept that provision in the crime bill, and finally they watched it being signed in the Rose Garden at the White House. He said that now gun control opponents were returning, and the situation was like the bully on a corner who is beaten up but always makes his way to another corner. Basically he was saying that nothing is getting done in this country. Everyone is using vituperative rhetoric to make themselves feel good and get their constituents riled up, but nothing is getting done in a positive way.

The President and Newt Gingrich recently met in New Hampshire. They were very polite to each other, talking civilly and rationally about difficult issues such as Medicare. Now they are back to name-calling again. Gingrich was quoted as saying that the Republicans like individual citizens who can do what is right and the President obviously likes bureaucrats who can use the citizens' money to do what they think is right. What malarkey! One way or another, citizens have to respond.

I refuse to participate in local talk shows until they begin researching and understanding the facts. Some people argue that a rational voice needs to be heard to confront purveyors of nonsense. I would rather forget them, but I'm afraid that in this society, forgetting them is simply not going to work, and thus sharp confrontation is inevitable.

QUESTION: What about the necessity of encouraging small businesses? I believe they are the backbone of local government revenue. The regulatory burden and taxes that discourage small businesses from hiring needs to be sharply reduced. Many of them won't hire permanent employees because they cannot afford to do so because of the taxes and regulation. Do you have a remedy for that problem?

MR. ABRAMSON: Obviously, there needs to be a rational balance regarding regulations. I have had trouble with the Occupational Safety and Health Administration (OSHA), for example. In one of the Carolina states a few years ago a fire broke out in a chicken processing plant, and because all of the doors were locked, employees could not escape. The OSHA requirement of a certain number of exits for a facility was not responded to, and as a result many people died. A rational approach must be found.

When I worked in the Kentucky governor's cabinet 15 years ago, Congress had just passed a law requiring mining companies to return the mountain to its original contour after they had strip-mined the coal from the top of the mountain. That law makes a great deal of sense except in a state such as Kentucky where the people greatly need flat land for new housing or shopping centers. Members of the governor's staff had to go to Washington to argue with the regulators about how their regulation needed to have some flexibility. A reality check must be made from time to time.

Another example is the Environmental Protection Agency (EPA) regulation of the recycling of inner-city land. Because of the demolished buildings that had lead-based paint, some land is contaminated with lead. If the land is going to be used as a child care facility, then it certainly should be cleaned up. If a slab of cement is going to be laid and a building put on top of it for manufacturing, however, the same standard of cleanliness should not be expected. These over-zealous EPA regulators look at me as if I am crazy when I make that point.

I am concerned, and I think the people of this nation are concerned, about clean water and clean air. My city has a real problem with air quality, and thus that concern is shared by the people living in Louisville. The government needs to strive for balance and some kind of reality check to assess whether a program is reasonable, appropriate, and cost-effective in terms of the potential risk involved.

You are right in your concern for small-business people, who create about 60 percent of the jobs in this nation. The political strength of the small-business associations in this country was seen when they were suddenly told that they might have to pay for government-mandated health care for their employees during the debate over the Clinton administration's proposal for national health care. Interestingly, Clinton saw health care as a problem, and the Republicans did not see it as a problem. Now the Republicans have decided that a health care crisis really does exist in the United States and a way must be found to solve the problem. This example again points to the need for rational dialogue. Without question, a health care problem does exist. Clinton probably overregulated it, and the Republicans probably underregulated it. One way or another, health care costs must be confronted and controlled. If helping the small businesses is so important, however, why do the Republicans want to eliminate the Small Business Administration (SBA)? SBA loans have been critical for the expansion of small businesses throughout this nation, yet the Republicans' proposal would leave small-business people to fend for themselves in raising the capital funds needed to help them succeed.

All of the issues you raised are difficult. I do not have specific solutions for them, but I do know that rational discussion is needed. Somewhere in the middle of the Chamber of Commerce's point of view and the left-liberal advocate's point of view, a meeting of the minds needs to occur to ensure a stronger economy for the future of America.

NARRATOR: Thank you, Mr. Abramson, for providing a fresh perspective on the difficult issue of the budget deficit.

II

THE ORIGINS AND GROWTH OF

THE DEFICIT AND THE DEBT

« CHAPTER 4 »

THE ORIGINS OF
THE BALANCED BUDGET IDEA
IN AMERICAN POLITICS*

JAMES D. SAVAGE

NARRATOR: James Savage is widely recognized as the person on the Government Department faculty, and quite possibly the entire University, with the most outstanding credentials in the study of the federal budget and budgeting process. He has two bachelor's degrees and one master's degree in political science from the University of California, Riverside, and a master's degree in public policy and another in economics from the University of California, Berkeley. He also has a doctorate from the University of California, Riverside, where he worked with an exacting committee that included Nelson Polsby, Aaron Wildavsky, Allan Sindler, and James Pierce.

Professor Savage won the Harold D. Lasswell Dissertation Award from the American Political Science Association. His book *Balanced Budgets and American Politics* (1988) was chosen by *Choice* magazine as the outstanding academic book selection for 1988-89. He received an Everett Dirksen Congressional Research Grant and was an Olin and Bradley postdoctoral fellow at Harvard. He

---

*Presented in a Forum at the Miller Center of Public Affairs on 11 July 1995.

continues to teach and write on American budgets and fiscal policy. We are very fortunate that he has kindly consented to discuss that subject today.

MR. SAVAGE: Rather than discussing the contemporary policy debates, I want to focus on the underlying reasons for the American preoccupation with balancing the budget. I submit that people should be skeptical of some explanations. For example, many Americans are concerned about the federal budget deficit because of its supposed upward effect on interest rates and inflation. There is very little evidence to suggest, in fact, that such relationships exist. For instance, the University sponsored a conference last April that included Bill Niskanen, a member of President Reagan's Council of Economic Advisers, and other prominent economists. They all agreed, despite their widely different perspectives, that little relation between deficits and interest rates exists. Milton Friedman, a monetarist who won the Nobel Prize, has openly claimed that there is no direct relationship between deficits and inflation or interest rates. Nevertheless, he does support balancing the budget and favors a constitutional amendment to do so because he wants to control the size of government.

When viewed in a comparative perspective, American deficits are relatively smaller than those of most other countries. During the 1970s and 1980s, for example, Belgium, Italy, Netherlands, the United Kingdom, Japan, Canada, and Australia had larger deficits as a percentage of their GDPs. The last time the U.S. budget was balanced was in 1969, yet Australia has outdone the United States, having run deficits each year between 1953 and 1987 (they resumed running deficits in 1990). Between 1970 and 1980 the average Japanese general account deficit was 3.7 percent of their total economy, while their deficits averaged about 24 percent of total government expenditures. In essence, they borrowed about a quarter of their budget. At the same time, the U.S. deficit stood at only about 2.1 percent of GDP and 9.7 percent of government outlays.

Not only have other countries run deficits for a much longer time, their political discourse does not reflect the obsession with balancing the budget that Americans seem to have. One reason

Americans talk about the need to balance the budget is because of the issue of intergenerational burden. Other countries have inter-generational burdens too, but they still run deficits, and they do not talk about deficits in the same way. Likewise, Americans make constant use of the analogy between balancing their personal check-books and the federal deficit; yet even though people in these other countries have checkbooks, they do not debate the budget in such a metaphorical context. Thus, I am suggesting that there is perhaps something unique about the American concern for balancing the budget. Fifteen years have passed since Ronald Reagan was elected president, yet the issue of balancing the budget still fills American newspapers and day-to-day discussions. This controversy can of course be traced back well before Ronald Reagan's presidency.

Historically, the sources of American concerns with balancing the budget have been primarily political rather than economic. The first major case of deficit spending in America occurred in 1690, when the Massachusetts Bay Colony found itself unable to pay the militia it had raised to fight the Indians. At that time, the standard currency consisted of gold and silver coins, but since there were no gold or silver mines in Massachusetts, Virginia, or any of the colonies, the only way the colonies could raise more money was through foreign trade. Massachusetts simply did not have enough gold and silver to pay the militia troops, and they threatened to storm the capitol building if not paid. To avoid a revolt, Massachusetts reverted to the equivalent of deficit spending and began issuing paper money called "bills of credit," which were circulating government securities that paid interest and principal. The colonial government convinced people to hold its paper money by promising them favorable interest rates. These bills of credit, however, represented an encumbrance on future revenues. The colonial government was wagering that sufficient gold and silver coins could be collected during the next tax cycle to pay off people who held these bills of credit and that this expectation would persuade people to regard this money as legitimate currency.

Bills of credit were used in every English colony in the New World. For example, between 1702 and 1716 Massachusetts had admitted over £5,000 of bills; South Carolina had admitted £90,000 by 1717 and £210,000 by 1736. Virginia began using bills of credit in 1755. Early on, such deficit spending became a part of American political life. Benjamin Franklin became successful as a printer by obtaining the contract to print the bills of credit for Pennsylvania.

The use of these bills of credit became quite extensive, given that the growing economy required an expanding money supply. Without enough money in circulation, people find it difficult to engage in economic transactions. At that time, there were no banks in colonial America. There were money lenders but no real financial system. Thus, the colonies would often resort to expanding their paper money supply, a form of deficit financing that rested on the hope that future taxation could pay off the debt.

Deficit financing became an issue in colonial relationships with England, and it was one of the reasons for the Revolutionary War. The colonists resented what they saw as an infringement upon their rights to engage in deficit spending. Considering the prominence of bills of credit in colonial America, it is not surprising that they likewise became one of the primary sources of funding the Revolutionary War. The "Continental" paper currency authorized by the Continental Congress in 1776 was in fact a bill of credit.

There were also disadvantages to using bills of credit, however. Every colony had its own kind of paper money that may or may not have been accepted in other colonies, potentially hampering intercolonial trade. Some colonies were irresponsible in allowing too many of these bills of credit, which would cause an inflated currency and create a great deal of tension between creditors and debtors. Nevertheless, it was a form of finance that was used throughout the colonial era, and it helped finance the Revolution.

After the Revolutionary War the states began to admit even larger sums of bills of credit, which was one factor that led to the Continental Convention in Philadelphia. In the introduction to Madison's *Notes*, he complains that state legislators were emitting too many bills of credit. Direct democracy had taken over in the state governments, and the lower houses of the legislatures had become very powerful, while many of the governor's powers had been greatly weakened. With no strong central authority to restrain them, state legislatures were extremely prone to admit bills of credit, often against the desires of creditors.

Article 12 of the Articles of Confederation had pledged the public's good faith to redeem "all bills of credit emitted, monies borrowed, and debt contracted by or under the authority of Congress. . . ." At the Constitutional Convention in 1787, one of the key questions was how to deal with these inflationary bills of credit. One draft version of the Constitution dated 6 August included Article 7, Section I, which provided for the authority "to borrow money and admit bills on the credit of the United States," in effect institutionalizing the national government's power to use bills of credit to borrow. This was the primary method of deficit spending.

A rather lengthy debate over this provision took place on 16 August 1787 after Gouvernor Morris made a motion to strike out the section on emitting bills of credit. Some people nowadays contend that the Founding Fathers never considered whether to have a balanced budget amendment, but this debate shows that in fact they did. Oliver Ellsworth, later a Supreme Court justice, stated that

> this is a favorable moment to shut and bar the door against paper money. The mischiefs of the various experiments which have been made are now fresh in the public mind and excitedly discussed of all the respectable part of America. By withholding the power from the new government more friends of influence be gained to it than by almost anything else. Paper money can in no case be necessary. Give the government credit and other resources will offer it. The power may do harm, never good.

One delegate commented that "the words [bills of credit], if not struck out, would be as alarming as the mark of the Beast in Revelation." The delegates agreed to get rid of bills of credit, primarily to attract "people of influence"—creditors and money lenders—to support the Constitution.

Also present at this convention was James Madison, an ally of Alexander Hamilton and a supporter of strong national government. In order to become strong, Hamilton claimed, national governments must have the ability to engage in deficit spending. Madison therefore downplayed the importance of this issue. In his *Notes* on the Convention, he recalled:

> The vote in the affirmative by Virginia was occasioned by the acquiescence of Mr. Madison, who became satisfied that striking out the words would not disable the government from the use of public notes as far as it could be safe and proper. It would only cut off the pretext for paper currency and in particular from making bills either a tender for public or private debts.

In essence, Madison agreed to the prohibition of bills of credit because of their inflationary capacity as a paper money, but only on the condition that there be no limit to the government's power to borrow through such means as promissory notes. The convention accepted this compromise.

At the same time, the delegates quickly passed a motion to strike out the use of bills of credit by state governments. The central issue involved not so much whether there should be deficit spending, as which level of government would have the authority to do so. As the leading advocate of centralized political authority (since Hamilton was absent from the convention at the time), Madison did everything he could to ensure that the federal government would have the power to borrow and sought to constrain the states' ability to borrow.

This became an issue during the ratification debates of the Constitution. At the Virginia Convention, Patrick Henry warned against the serious consequences of eliminating the power of borrowing at the state level. A delegate named Locke at the North Carolina convention said:

> I wish those gentlemen who made those observations would consider the necessity which compels us a great measure to make such money. Necessity compelled them to pass the law in order to save the vast numbers of people from ruin. I hope to be excused and observant that it would have been hard for the late Continental Army to lay down the arms which with they had valiantly and successfully fought for their country without receiving or being promised and assured some sort of compensation for their past services. What a situation this country would have been

in if they had the power over the person's sword. This state cannot air proportioned specie [which was gold and silver]. To have laid down a tax for that purpose would have been oppressive. What was to be done? The only expedient was to pass a law to make paper money and to make it a tender.

At three of the states' ratification conventions, provisions were passed that would strike the federal government's power to borrow any money at all. In New York, Gilbert Livingston proposed an amendment that said, "No money may be borrowed with the credit of the United States without the assent of two-thirds of the senators and representatives present in each House." Rhode Island supported Livingston's position. Of course, none of these proposals were incorporated into the Constitution.

Therefore, by the time George Washington became president, there was already a long history of deficit spending by the colonial governments, the state governments, and the national government. The issue of deficit spending, although it had economic undertones, clearly centered around questions of political power. England did not want the colonies to engage in deficit spending because it might affect trade issues and relationships between the colonial governments. Likewise, the federal government wanted to constrain the state governments and therefore Article 1, Section 10 of the Constitution prohibited the states from emitting bills of credit. Later on, the federal government would in fact use constitutional authority to borrow money by way of promissory notes and other financial securities.

After the Constitutional Convention, George Washington was elected as the first president and chose Alexander Hamilton, Thomas Jefferson's nemesis, as the secretary of the treasury. Hamilton issued a number of historically influential reports that articulated the important role of national political power in promoting the economy. He proposed a number of solutions to the economic difficulties facing the federal government, burdened as it was with more than $50 million in debt, an enormous amount of money at the time. It was Hamilton's job to manage this national debt, and in 1790 he issued "The Report Relative to a Provision for the Support of Public Credit." In that report, he explained:

> That exigencies are to be expected to occur in the affairs of
> nations in which there will be a necessity for borrowing; that loans
> in times of public danger, especially from foreign war, are found
> in indispensable resource, even to the wealthiest of them. And
> that in a country, which, like this, is possessed of little active
> wealth, or in other words, little monied capital, the necessity for
> that resource, must, in such emergencies, be proportionately
> urgent.

Hamilton basically argued that government has to borrow not only
in times of war but also in times of public danger. He borrowed his
economic policy proposals from several sources. From Adam
Smith's *The Wealth of Nations* he borrowed the idea of a national
bank. He borrowed from David Hume's essay, *On Public Credit*, the
idea that public debt could in fact promote the economy.

Thomas Jefferson expressed extreme hostility to Hamilton's call
for deficit spending and borrowing. In an essay written in February
1818, Jefferson says:

> Hamilton was indeed a singular character of acute understanding,
> disinterested, honest, and honorable in all private transaction in a
> society and in private life and so bewitched and perverted by the
> British example as to be under the thorough conviction that
> corruption is essential to the government of a nation.

Later, Jefferson added, "Hamilton's financial system had two
objects—first as a puzzle to exclude popular understanding and
inquiry; second, as a machine for the corruption of the legislature."
Furthermore, Jefferson claimed, "I know well it must be so
understood that nothing like a majority of Congress had yielded to
this corruption—far from it, but a division not equal had already
taken place in the honest part of that body." Jefferson was
referring to the scheme for financing the national debt that
Hamilton had set up as secretary of the treasury—a large centralized
economic policy structure that included the Bank of the United
States. Hamilton advocated the promotion of the nation's economy
through the use of tariffs to encourage domestic manufacturing,
while using these tariffs to fiance the nation's deficit spending.
Handling all of these finances would require a larger Treasury

Department with more bureaucrats, which caused Jefferson to become extremely concerned. The government's deficits and debt, and the Bank and tariffs used to finance this debt, Jefferson charged, would "corrupt" the republic.

The emphasis on corruption was a central theme of Jefferson's political thinking. Just as Hamilton borrowed certain ideas from David Hume and Adam Smith, Jefferson borrowed concepts from English political thought and applied them to the American experience. From Viscount Bolingbroke and the English Whigs came the concept of corruption, which in turn was borrowed from Machiavelli and ancient Greek political thought. The belief was that excessive public debt would undermine the constitutional balance of powers in a government because the ministers, rather than the king or members of Parliament, would become increasingly powerful and independent.

Following the Glorious Revolution of 1688, England accumulated a huge debt because of war-related expenses. The English government, lacking a centralized banking system, established the Bank of London to handle its wartime debt. In effect, the debt was farmed out—people could buy into the debt, and the rapidly growing speculation in English debt led to something called "The South Seas Bubble Crisis" (1720) in which numerous wealthy people, including royalty, went bankrupt. The prime minister at the time, Walpole, and his ministers were using the public debt to influence elections and reward political allies. Many in the aristocracy opposed this new centralization of power, which they viewed as destroying the traditional constitutional framework in England. This accumulation of public debt and its manipulation by ministers, the expansion of the civil lists of the bureaucracy to manage it, and the growing industrialized economy that depended on ample credit all fit under the label *corruption.*

Jefferson borrowed this notion and saw in Hamilton's plans exactly what had happened in England a century before. He therefore strongly opposed the centralization of the economy via the Bank of the United States, the promotion of a manufacturing economy through high-tariff protectionism, and the federal government's involvement in projects such as canal building that he thought were beyond its constitutional authority. He was likewise highly suspicious of the expansion of the national debt and Hamilton's willingness to borrow not just in time of war, but in times of public danger. In the expansion of the Treasury Department and the growth of the federal bureaucracy, Jefferson saw England's corruption taking root in America.

As compared to Hamilton's vision for an industrialized America, Jefferson advocated an agrarian vision that would control corruption. In his *Notes on the State of Virginia*, he writes:

> Corruption of morals and the mass of cultivators is a phenomenon which no age nor nation is furnished an example. Any proportion of which the aggregate of the other classes of citizens bears any state that its husbandmen is a proportion of its unsound healthy parts is of good enough nature whereby to measure its degree of corruption.

Elsewhere, he compares the United States with Europe in a letter to Madison:

> This reliance on the people cannot deceive us as long as we remain virtuous, and I think we shall be so, so long as agriculture is our principal object, which will be in the case while there remains vacant lands in any part of America. We can pile upon one another in large cities as in Europe where we shall become as corrupt as in Europe and go to eating one another as they do there.

In other words, he saw Hamilton's economic policy of federal budget deficits and mounting debt as a vehicle to realize Hamilton's dream of a manufacturing economy, which Jefferson opposed emphatically.

In sharp contrast, Jefferson believed that deficit spending at the state level was acceptable because it did not have the same kind of corrupting effect on the public. Jefferson's philosophy embodied an interesting paradox. Whereas he suggested that the national government's debts represented the source of corruption, the decentralized nature of the state governments prevented such corruption. In 1798, Jefferson wrote in a letter to his friend John Taylor:

I wish it were possible to obtain a single amendment to our Constitution. I would be willing to depend upon on that alone the reduction of the administration of our government for the genuine principles of its Constitution. I mean an additional article taking from the federal government the power for borrowing. I now deny their power of making money or anything else of legal tender. I know that to pay all proper expenses within the year would in case of war be hard on us, but not so hard as ten wars instead of one, for wars would be reduced in proportion. Besides that, the state governments will be free to lend their credit in borrowing quotas. It is a singular phenomenon that while our state governments are the very best in the world without exception or comparison, our general government has in the rapid course of nine or ten years become more arbitrary and has swallowed more the public liberty than even that of England.

Of course, Jefferson believed that Hamilton would have a different perspective. He wrote to George Washington, "This exactly marks the difference between Colonel Hamilton's views and mine, that I would wish the debt paid tomorrow. He wishes it never to be paid, but always to be a thing wherewith to corrupt and manage the legislature."

Jefferson's letter is fascinating. Unlike Hamilton, who supported federal borrowing in *any* time of public danger, Jefferson opposed federal borrowing even in case of outright war. Jefferson advocated an agrarian economy. Jefferson did not oppose all deficit spending; he just opposed federal deficit spending in favor of state borrowing. Hamilton, meanwhile, favored federal deficit spending while opposing state deficit spending. The underlying issue dividing the two men was political power, not mere economics. Notwithstanding his quote to Madison that people would pile up on each other and be corrupt as in European cities, after becoming president, Jefferson himself borrowed money for the Louisiana Purchase to maintain his agrarian vision for America. This was the only time Jefferson engaged in borrowing, while running budget surpluses in all but one year of his presidency.

The Jacksonians kept alive the notion of corruption. Andrew Jackson proclaimed, "We shall then exhibit the rare example of a great nation abounding in all the means of happiness and security altogether free from debt." Jackson shared Jefferson's political thinking about deficits, which points to the lasting power of political ideas. Until the Civil War, this notion of corruption continued to predominate in political language related to balancing the federal budget. Keep in mind that the White House is the source of much of our political rhetoric and political ideas. Under the leadership of Jackson, the United States came closer than at any other time in U.S. history to eliminating completely the public debt. Spending restraint by the national government and a fairly strong economy enabled the United States to pay off the national debt in 1836, only to have it grow again after a bank panic in 1837.

Jackson faced the same kind of political opposition from advocates of centralized government as Jefferson did. Jackson and Jefferson believed in limited government and in reducing the government's financial powers, which meant balancing budgets. Just as Hamilton had called for strengthening the economy, Daniel Webster and Henry Clay advocated the "American System"—a proposal to use the federal government's deficits to promote the economy. Webster and Clay wanted government to spend money on bridges, roads, harbors, and other forms of infrastructure. To avoid excessive deficits, the government would have to raise tariffs, which in turn would promote manufacturing to the detriment of agriculture. This became one of the major issues that heightened tensions prior to the Civil War. The South bitterly resented high tariffs, which in effect transferred wealth from the agriculture sector to the manufacturing sector centered in the North.

Jackson directly confronted Hamilton's legacy—the Bank of the United States, the centralized source of financial power in America, which had the unintended consequence of promoting state deficits and debt. In 1832 Jackson vetoed the bill to renew the charter of the Bank of the United States, which had served as a device to constrain state deficit spending. Even though Article I, Section 10 of the Constitution prohibited the states from emitting bills of credit, states circumvented that restriction by promoting state-chartered banks, which emitted their own paper money. This method did not violate the Constitution because the paper money was issued by the *banks*, not the state governments. Without the Bank of the United States to control them, state banks were able to extend as much credit as they desired. From 1835 to 1838, the state governments borrowed more—$107 million—than all of the federal deficits between 1789 and 1838, which totalled $99.7 million. The point is that although the American political consciousness at this time regarded federal spending as bad, state deficits were deemed permissible. It was not until after the states began defaulting on their debts in the wake of the bank panic of 1837 that they enacted their own balanced budget requirements. In 1842, Rhode Island became the first state to restrict its own deficit spending. Virginia did not enact such a provision until 1870. Of course, states found a way to get around their own constitutions through various kinds of bonds. Before the Civil War, Virginia was the largest state debtor, and had it not been for Virginia's massive issue of bonds for building railroads and other infrastructure used by the Confederacy, the Civil War might well have been of shorter duration.

Thus, America has a unique historical tradition of concern for budget balancing that dates back to Thomas Jefferson. The tradition has origins in English political thought, and it has been manifested over the years in controversies over state versus federal control over the economy and in debates over the proper role of budgeting. Budgeting is always primarily political. It involves questions of who has what kind of power and what will be the function of government in society. The concern of some Americans for balancing the budget reflects their concerns about excessively centralized political authority. It is very important for the American people to recognize the historical and political tradition underlying this debate.

QUESTION: Was the interest rate in bills of credit issued by states implicit or explicit? What was the rate of colonial inflation? You mentioned that many countries have run budget deficits for decades, whereas little data is available about countries that have taken constructive efforts to reduce their deficits. Is it therefore difficult to make conclusions on the expected benefits of reducing deficits?

MR. SAVAGE: First, bills of credit varied between colonies and states. Sometimes the interest was explicit, and sometimes it was written in some provision. The only way colonial governments could persuade people to hold bills of credit was through the implicit if not explicit promise that they would receive a greater return. Inflation rates varied widely among the colonies because each colony had control of its own money supply. The colonies experienced many boom-and-bust cycles that were heavily related to the Indians wars, the French and Indian Wars, and especially the effect of European conflicts on shipbuilding.

Regarding the second issue concerning the lack of sufficient data, economists tend to be closely tied to the ideology and the worldview of the professors who trained them. Because of these strong attachments, it is rare when a roomful of economists manage to agree with each other on a particular issue. Some economists, for example, assert that changes in deficits have no effect on interest rates or inflation, citing data going back to the Civil War.

Again, this dispute highlights the preeminence of politics in these economic debates. For instance, Ronald Reagan claimed that deficits do not cause high interest rates or inflation, but this was because he believed that the government had to be restrained. He would not admit that deficits were so bad that higher taxes were needed because for him raising taxes meant perpetuating big government.

Interestingly, Bill Clinton says deficits do cause high interest rates. A Keynesian economist or anyone who believes that deficits have a positive effect on the economy must also accept the notion that above some level, deficits will produce a negative effect on the economy. Clinton, of course, opposes a balanced budget amendment, though he has also called for a balanced budget. His problem is in a sense more complex than Reagan's: To defend the government's activist role in the economy, he must defend deficit spending in principle, even as he attacks specific deficits in practice. That agenda is difficult to sell to the public.

MR. GEORGE McKINNEY: I appreciate your awareness of the political issues involved, but frankly I think you are in serious error when you talk about economists and their policy positions. A survey by the National Association of Business Economists asked its members whether or not they agreed with the philosophies represented by William Niskanen and Milton Friedman, and 87 percent of them disagreed. Also, contrary to what you say, I have found that the number of economists who find little or no correlation between deficits and inflation is very small. The South American syndrome of deficits financed by printing or borrowing money demonstrates that this practice has led to unstable political systems and has had highly inflationary impact on South American economies. There is no way a deficit can be increased without having a significant impact on the economy in one way or another. Inevitably, there will be a decline in the national savings rate, followed by higher inflation, a slower rate of growth, or the sale of substantial parts of our national assets to foreigners.

MR. SAVAGE: My point is that the economics profession is not united. A variety of schools of thought have identified little or no systematic effect from the deficit. I want to emphasize the political aspect of these economic debates.

At a conference at the University in April 1994, I asked Bill Niskanen about the relationship between deficits and interests rates. Niskanen said that Clinton made a mistake by claiming that lowering the deficit would lead to lower interest rates. There is very little evidence suggesting that federal borrowing or even combined government sector borrowing has had any significant effect on interest rates. Robert Eisner, the past president of the American Economic Association, agreed almost completely with Bill Niskanen on this issue, despite his sharp difference in perspective. Eisner also talks about how, in fact, deficits promote investment and savings.

One can go though the economics profession and find many prestigious people making these kinds of comments. In 1979 the deficit was less than $30 billion. If it were that low today, it would be cause for rejoicing. If someone had predicted in 1979 that there would be national deficits of $200 billion or more for a decade but with inflation rates equivalent to those of the early 1960s, that person would have been called a lunatic. When federal deficits first reached $100 billion, people were talking about 20 percent interest rates and inflation rates. Clinton is the first president since Harry Truman to have declining budget deficits for three consecutive years. Nevertheless, the Federal Reserve Board has increased interest rates since 1992. Likewise, in spite of the imminent passage of a rescission bill of $17 billion and the Republican resolution to balance the budget in seven years, the Fed has lowered interest rates by a mere quarter of a percent. Thus, there are grounds for legitimate skepticism about the claimed relationship between deficits and the economy.

MR. McKINNEY: A major source of confusion on this issue is the failure to distinguish between the immediate, short-run impacts of changes in monetary and fiscal policies on one hand and their long-run impacts on the other. There is a big difference.

QUESTION: What accounts for the dollar's 90 percent decline in purchasing power since the end of World War II? How did that decline occur if not because of deficit spending and the United States' huge debt accumulation?

MR. SAVAGE: Much has changed since World War II. The economies of other countries have developed and are no longer in shambles. The United States has had an active role in promoting other economies. In addition, other countries employ their own monetary and fiscal policies to promote their own currencies. The dollar's decline in value relative to German and Japanese currencies has much to do with interest rate policies of their central banks in recent years. America has declined as an economic superpower, relatively speaking, in part because other economies have grown. There are many reasons for the dollar's decline.

NARRATOR: When the Miller Center began this series on the deficit problem, Alan Murray urged us to give voice to different points of view. We have certainly had a lively debate today. Professor Savage has fully established his credentials in the field, and we thank him for his informative presentation.

« CHAPTER 5 »

THE FEDERAL BUDGET DEFICIT: AN EXERCISE IN HYPOCRISY*

GEORGE W. McKINNEY, JR.

NARRATOR: George McKinney is Virginia Bankers Association Chair Professor Emeritus at the McIntire School of Commerce. Earlier, he was senior vice president of Irving Trust and prior to that a financial economist and manager of the Discount and Credit Department of the Federal Reserve Bank in Richmond.

Mr. McKinney was born in Amigo, West Virginia. He graduated from Berea College and earned his master's and doctoral degrees at the University of Virginia. He also studied at the Stonier Graduate School of Banking at Rutgers University where he taught for 13 years. In addition, he has taught at various national and state schools of banking and has been very active in the American Bankers Association. It is a pleasure to welcome him to the Miller Center.

MR. McKINNEY: I recently read an interesting article in a professional journal which said that, from an economic point of view, federal budget deficits do not really make any difference. Much of the argument was based on the fact that inflation and interest rates

---

Presented in a Forum at the Miller Center of Public Affairs on 15 August 1995.

do not always seem to be correlated. From my personal experience, my professional experience, and my understanding of economic theory, I would expect deficits, inflation, and interest rates *not* to move in the same direction all the time. In the middle of a depression, inflation and interest rates are likely to be low, and that is when one would also expect budget deficits to be high. In an inflationary period, interest rates are always high, and that is when the budget ought to be in surplus. I would expect there to be different relationships among deficits and interest rates, depending on whether inappropriate fiscal policies were a major cause of the inflation or depression, or whether appropriate fiscal policies were being used to offset the inflation or depression.

Our economy is obviously much too complicated for us to expect simple one-to-one relationships between important economic variables. Interest rates and deficits reflect and are reflected in every aspect of our day-to-day life. Many other factors are involved as well, and we need to be aware of how they affect the deficit, inflation, interest rates, and overall economic activity. You cannot just tie the two variables together and let it go at that.

Approximately a century ago, a man by the name of Alfred Marshall used a bowl of marbles to illustrate the basic economic truth that economic forces are constantly competing with each other as they move toward a general equilibrium that represents the optimal relationship among all of the players in the economic game. He pointed out that if one marble is moved, the others will have to adjust to the new situation; the more marbles moved, the bigger the impact of each move.

The Congressional Budget Office (CBO) recently estimated that the United States will have a deficit of nearly $200 billion next year, which is a lot of marbles. It is equivalent to 3 percent of everything produced in the United States. If three marbles are taken from or added to the bowl, the whole marble arrangement must change. If a tax cut is enacted while the budget deficit is 3 percent of gross national product (GNP), the nation's income will not be the same size it would have been otherwise, and it will not be distributed in the same way. Those marbles will have settled down in a different way. We can thus begin our discussion secure in the knowledge that the deficit makes a big economic difference. The real question is, What is that difference?

Since Marshall's day, economists have come to view economic activity as being a smooth continuum. In other words, the economy does not respond to the movement of one marble and then sit and wait for another marble to be moved. All of the marbles are constantly moving. Marshall was right about one thing, however— our economy is constantly moving toward equilibrium. It just never gets there because too many new things are happening. Our thinking about the budget deficit needs to be flexible enough to allow for as many new things as possible.

Politicians deal with deficits in fascinating ways. Some of their methods are unintentional, but many of them in recent years strike me as pure hypocrisy. In 1932 Franklin Roosevelt campaigned actively on a platform that promised a balanced budget. Yet after taking office, FDR ran peacetime deficits that averaged 3.5 percent of the nation's total output; at one point it reached 4.5 percent. During Jimmy Carter's four years in the White House the deficit jumped to 3 percent of total output, the highest by a wide margin since World War II. Ronald Reagan expressed deep concern over the $80 billion deficit and the national debt which was rapidly approaching one trillion dollars. During the campaign of 1980 he promised to slow the growth of spending, cut taxes, and balance the budget by 1983. After he was elected he did indeed cut taxes, but spending jumped from just over 22 percent of national output to nearly 24.5 percent. By the time he left office in 1989, the national debt had tripled and was rapidly approaching $3 trillion. Reagan's budget deficits averaged $176 billion, which was more than twice the record $80 billion deficit he inherited from Carter. During FDR's pump-priming New Deal years, the highest budget deficit was 4.5 percent of national output. Reagan's deficits *averaged* 4.4 percent, and reached a peak level of 6 percent! Reagan's administration blamed those continuing large deficits on a spendthrift Congress. Actually, total government spending for each of those eight years was within 1 percent of the budget totals that were originally proposed by the Reagan administration.

In 1986 Senators Phil Gramm, Warren Rudman, and Ernest Hollings pushed through legislation mandating cuts in federal spending and promised that the new law would cut $108 billion from the deficit by 1991. As it turned out, the deficit did *not* decline; it rose from $150 billion in 1987 to $270 billion in 1991. While George Bush was campaigning for the Republican presidential nomination in 1980, he referred to Reagan's fiscal policy proposals as "voodoo economics." Apparently ignoring his own past rhetoric, however, Bush expanded the annual deficit each year by more than $100 billion during his four years in office, and the national debt climbed from nearly $3 trillion to $4.4 trillion. Bill Clinton recently put forth a plan to balance the budget by 2005, but according to Congressional Budget Office reports, the President's figures do not add up to a balanced budget. CBO findings indicate that Clinton's proposals would leave a $209 billion deficit in 2005, a little higher than it is now.

The biggest hypocrisy in the balanced budget debate, though, stems from the general public, particularly the opinion leaders who help shape public policy. Personal experience and common sense tell us that large and persistent borrowing under most circumstances will weaken the nation, yet citizens do not demand that their senators and representatives take positive action to reduce it. Furthermore, when asked to take a cut in benefits or tax breaks that each of us receives from government, people complain bitterly. Californians and Texans do not want the budget to be balanced by closing their military bases. Virginians do not want the budget to be balanced by eliminating peanut and tobacco subsidies. Wealthy individuals do not want the budget to be balanced by raising taxes on their capital gains. Oldsters do not want the budget to be balanced by reducing their Social Security and Medicare benefits.

Former Senate Majority Leader Sam Rayburn once said, "Don't tax you; don't tax me. Tax that fellow behind the tree!" Nowadays people say, "Don't cut my benefits. Let's balance the budget in someone else's back yard!" Wouldn't it be nice if that article I read had it right and we really could get all of those benefits without bothering to pay for them?

The effects of deficits are several. First, there is a virtual knee-jerk relationship between the size of the deficit and the actions of the Federal Reserve System. If the economy is moving along at a comfortable pace and a large tax cut adds three marbles to our bowl, the Fed will automatically take three marbles out! That is what we hired them to do. The problem is, the marbles get jumbled up in the process because the deficit marbles do not enter the bowl in the same place that the Fed's marbles came out. Depending on the nature of the tax cut, someone's after-tax income is bound to increase sharply. Those who benefit from the tax cut will spend more, but the government will not spend any less. Therefore, the immediate effect of a tax cut is an increase in overall spending.

In contrast, the Fed can only do its job by restraining credit so that people are forced to cut back on their borrowing. When the Fed tightens credit, interest rates always rise—not necessarily higher than they were before, but higher than they would have been if the Fed had not been obliged to tighten credit.

In an ideal world, the government's fiscal policy and the Fed's monetary policy would work hand in glove to help achieve an economic environment favorable to a stable economy and a rising standard of living. Either fiscal policy or monetary policy can stimulate the economy, and likewise, either can slow it down. If fiscal policy is overly stimulative, however, as it has been for the past couple of decades, then the Fed is duty bound to offset that stimulus. If the Fed does what we hire them to do, interest rates are going to be higher than they would have otherwise been. My personal guess is that the current deficit may add as much as 2 percent to long-term borrowing costs. That increase means a great deal to businessmen and home buyers.

Other "marbles" adjust to a deficit created by a tax cut in different ways. Our particular interest concerns the effects of the deficit on long-term economic performance in this country. Consider first the basic relationship between national savings and the nation's stock of capital equipment. Capital formation is essential to economic growth. If the nation is to achieve economic growth, we have to sacrifice today by spending less of our income so that there will be a pool of savings with which to buy that capital equipment.

Our nation can access only five sources of funds for capital formation: savings by business—depreciation allowances and retained earnings; savings by individuals—not spending all of their current incomes; government surpluses; net exports; and borrowing from or selling assets to foreigners. Government surpluses provide savings in the same way personal savings do. Deficits, on the other hand, eat up savings from other parts of the economy. Taxes directly contribute to national saving because from an economic point of view, by definition, any income that is not spent is saved. We certainly do not spend the money that we pay in taxes.

In that context, the initial impact of a tax cut is essentially the same, no matter what the current economic environment is like. When taxes are cut, after-tax incomes always increase, and people spend more. No one spends any less; government spending is untouched by the tax cut, per se. As a result, total spending always increases when taxes are cut.

At the next level of secondary impacts, however, the resulting increase in spending can be either be good or bad, depending on the state of the economy. If the nation is in a depression, the extra demand for goods and services will be beneficial. As we buy more cars or shirts or computers, factories will need to increase their output and hire more workers. As the new workers earn more income, in turn, they will spend more money, and that keeps the circle going and helps pull us out of the depression.

Actually, taxing and spending policies automatically cushion the business cycle to some degree. During a recession, tax revenues fall while welfare and unemployment outlays rise, so that incomes decline less than they would otherwise have declined and the recession is not as severe as it would have been. During a boom, in contrast, tax collections rise, and these social benefit payments taper off. We call these effects "automatic stabilizers." Deficits and surpluses that are caused by these automatic stabilizers and discretionary countercyclical measures do not hurt us; they help smooth out the business cycle.

Those measures are in sharp contrast to the effect of deficits that occur when the economy is running at full tilt. If the economy is fully employed and tax cuts create or add to a deficit, the immediate impact is the same: a greater demand for goods and services. The output of goods and services does not increase, however, because our productive machine is already running at full tilt. Either people pay more for the goods they buy, which is called inflation, or they buy them from overseas.

GEORGE W. MCKINNEY, JR.

The Reagan administration described those deficits that continue year in and year out even when no such stimulus is appropriate as "structural deficits," as opposed to "cyclical deficits," which disappear at full employment of our resources. I think that is good terminology. As a general principle, cyclical deficits should be welcomed as helpful and structural deficits should be condemned. The technicians can argue the fine points of measurement—what ought to be included, what ought to be excluded, and whether a small structural deficit ought to be tolerated—but you and I, as informed members of the electorate, should press for a substantially balanced structural deficit as a fiscal policy objective. For instance, if your child has appendicitis, the appendix should be removed. Let the doctors argue about how to hold the scalpel, but get the appendix out! It is the same thing with this budget deficit.

In 1981 a very large tax cut created an unprecedented peacetime deficit. The Fed's initial reaction was to maintain a tight money policy, and necessarily so, or else inflation would have quickly gotten out of hand. Lots of marbles were put into the bowl, and lots of marbles were taken out of the bowl! The tax cut, of course, stimulated spending. In previous years, consumers had been spending 63 or 64 percent of the nation's income, but in recent years we have been consistently spending over 68 percent. A disproportionate amount of that increased spending went into purchases of imports from overseas.

Meanwhile, the tight money that was needed to offset this increased spending had the expected restraining influence. Actually, money had already been tightened in 1979 in response to the increase in the deficit under Carter. Monetary restraint shows up first in short-term interest rates, which shot up in 1981 above 20 percent. Since inflation was running at double-digit rates, long-term rates that were adjusted for inflation were still at moderately low levels. During the first four years of the Reagan administration when the deficit was rising sharply, however, long-term rates, after adjustment for inflation, more than doubled, from the 3 percent range to the 7 percent range. The deficit caused a tremendous jump in the total demand for credit for housing, consumer credit, business borrowing for capital investment, and government borrowing. The government received, as it always does, all of the credit it wanted, regardless of how high interest rates had to go. (We call that "necessitous borrowing.") The increased government borrowing, however, left a $200 billion shortfall for the private sector to cope with. Interest rates had to rise high enough to either squeeze the entire $200 billion out of private markets or attract new funds from somewhere else. That is where the overseas marble comes in.

The higher interest rates attracted large amounts of portfolio investments from overseas. At the same time, foreigners realized the long-term significance of that tax cut stimulus and they chose to invest in the upcoming U.S. spending boom. Many of their investments were in productive facilities—Japanese auto plants in Tennessee and Georgia, for example. Much of it was in inflation hedges—golf courses in Hawaii and Pebble Beach, real estate such as Rockefeller Center, and common stock equities, for example.

It is impossible to buy American real estate with pounds, deutschemarks, or yen. An overseas investor must buy the dollars with yen and then buy real estate with dollars. Consequently, the demand for dollars goes up, and the price of dollars is bid up on world markets. The dollar strengthens—not just by a little, but by a lot. At its peak in 1985, the trade-weighted dollar had gone up 75 percent, causing the price tag on American goods sold to jump by 75 percent, even though the number of dollars our businessmen get for each sale remains the same. This gave businessmen only three options: to cut prices nearly in half, accept a big drop in market share, or do some of both. Any choice made would cause financial loss, so the most commonly chosen alternative was to pull out of those markets.

Do you know that the United States does not have one single manufacturer of compact disc players? Zenith has gone out of the television-making business; it was the very last television manufacturer in the United States. The blame can be laid directly on the economic situation resulting from massive budget deficits. Our exports are much lower than they would have been otherwise. If the dollar strengthens by 75 percent, that is another way of saying that other currencies are 43 percent cheaper; it is an inverse relationship. When the price tag on everything foreigners sell in the United States drops by 43 percent, that gives them a tremendous competitive edge. It lets them take over a larger share of U.S. markets without touching their profit margins. In summary, the nation's exports plummet and imports skyrocket. By 1987, a nation that had once prided itself on its international competitiveness was buying $160 billion a year more than it could sell overseas. Our trade deficit is still running over $100 billion a year.

An interesting observation is that the foreign-investment marble and the trade-deficit marble are locked together mathematically. It is impossible to continue to buy more from foreign countries than they buy from the United States unless those countries either lend our country the money or buy some of its assets. In effect, Americans have been selling off U.S. assets to finance a domestic spending and importing spree.

Before those $200 billion budget deficits occurred, the United States was in the proud position of being the world's largest creditor. Its overseas investments were the envy of all nations and gave our country more muscle in its role as leader of the free world. (Borrowers do not often tell lenders what to do.) Now the United States is in the dubious position of being the world's largest debtor nation, well ahead of all those profligate Latin American countries we derisively call "banana republics" due to their inability to manage their finances. Therefore, the United States is having more trouble getting other nations to support its international initiatives.

Expectations are a big factor in any economic relationship, particularly in financial matters, because credit can be extended indefinitely as long as lenders have confidence in the borrower's creditworthiness. When the borrower is overspending his income by 3 percent year after year, however, that confidence could evaporate overnight. A foreign exchange trader once told me that the trick is to look the other trader in the eye, express supreme confidence in your market position, and watch for him to blink. When he does, you have to rush and sell before all the other traders. Foreign investors react the same way to the stock market. If investors think the market has room to go up, they are likely to buy, but if they think the market has about run out of steam, they want to get out ahead of everyone else. During 1929, 1974, and 1987, foreign investors became less confident in America's future economic strength and took the profits on their dollar holdings and converted them back into their own currencies or into some other currency they perceived to be strengthening. Currently, the pace of selling dollar assets is quickening, particularly in Japan.

Furthermore, our nation is becoming more vulnerable to losing its role in international finance as the world's largest repository for the official reserves of other nations. Ten years ago 70 percent of the world's official reserves were held in dollars; now it is 60 percent. This country inherited the international banking function from Great Britain after their continuing international payments deficits triggered a series of crises. The world's central banks came to feel that their banker at the time, England, was getting shaky so they found a new banker, the United States. In recent years, Germany has started to look more and more like the new bastion of financial stability. If Japan can shake off its current banking crisis, it will appear appealingly stable as well. The possibility that other nations will shift their official balances to one or both of these nations is a real one, and if that happens, our role as political leader of the free world will be further inhibited.

I do not know when global investors will sell their dollars. Most likely, there will be a sudden erosion of confidence in the dollar and a period of increasing difficulty in financing our overseas purchases. When on a slippery slope, as the United States is, one is never quite sure how far down the slope he is, but the farther down one gets, the more precarious the position. As our nation moves down that slope, foreign central banks start denominating their loans to people in *their* currencies, not in dollars. That would mean loans to the United States would have to be paid back in deutsche-marks or yen, and if the dollar continued to depreciate, it would take more dollars to pay off the same amount of debt. Private investors from overseas won't buy bonds denominated in dollars if this scenario continues to unfold. A case in point: Fannie Mae (FNMA, the Federal National Mortgage Association) recently issued bonds worth one billion deutschemarks ($720 million) to be sold on world markets. These bonds sold out in one hour because they were denominated in deutschemarks instead of dollars. The United States can probably stay on that slippery slope for some time and still be able to borrow, just as Mexico has done, but it may carry an increasingly steep interest-rate price tag.

The stakes in this argument are high. Our nation's growth will continue to lag as long as it has a large structural deficit. It simply will not have enough capital resources to invest. There is an important connection between our budget deficit, our trade deficit, and our heavy borrowing from foreign official institutions, which raises the very real possibility that these institutions will stiffen their lending terms and maybe take their reserve balances elsewhere. The important consideration is that the linkage also extends into the military and diplomatic fields, undermining our country's ability to be heard on important international issues. Our nation simply can not afford to take these risks.

What can we do about it? The Congress and the administration are playing around with several plans to balance the budget by the year 2000, 2002, or 2005, but none of them balances it by 1996 or 1997, which strikes me as a much more reasonable time frame. History has taught us that we cannot believe what our politicians say they are going to do about budget deficits. The longer the time frame, the more time politicians have to evade the issues and the more time they have to borrow and spend and borrow and spend. I do not believe, and I doubt if any of you believe, that spending is going to be cut by anything close to the amount needed to balance the budget. Our country's leaders need to stop playing games and get the nation's priorities in order.

Priority number one is to balance the budget and get rid of that structural deficit. Priority number two is to accomplish this by cutting spending to the maximum extent possible. The government needs to squeeze out as much waste, fraud, and mismanagement that the Congress and the administration can stomach. Take them at their word only *after* they deliver on past promises. Our third priority is to recognize that if the government cannot or will not balance the budget by cutting spending, then it should do it by raising taxes—certainly *not* by cutting taxes. That attempt failed abysmally during the 1980s.

It is simply a matter of basic honesty. Wiping out the deficit would release some $200 billion in national savings that could be used by the private economy for capital investment such as new homes, new plants and equipment. With more investments flowing into the stock of real capital, productive capacity would grow faster, the standard of living would improve accordingly, and I could stop apologizing to my grandchildren for wasting their birthright.

QUESTION: Would you continue raising the payroll tax, which is already the major tax on the middle class, on everyone?

MR. McKINNEY: The main task today is figuring out how to reduce the budget deficit. If the government will not cut spending, the nation will be greatly harmed. That leads to the question you are asking, which is, what kind of taxes should we raise? It is true that there would be different economic impacts, depending on which taxes were raised. Nevertheless, my same answer is: The tax that is raised does not matter nearly as much as *whether* we raise taxes. Payroll taxes on the middle class would be a productive way of increasing national saving, because middle-class people save a lower proportion of their incomes than do high-income or wealthy people. Therefore, if one were striving for a reduction in consumer spending, that would be a good way to accomplish it. The big thing plaguing our country today is excessive spending on imported goods and the need to increase capital investment here. Just reducing the deficit would do more to solve that problem than would any particular type of tax increase.

QUESTION: Assuming nothing is done and the current deficit continues, what will happen?

MR. McKINNEY: In the first place, the United States would fall off the slippery slope just as England did. Their position as unchallenged leader of the free world disappeared a couple of generations ago largely because of the same policy mistakes our country is making now. Our position as the unchallenged leader of the free world is in the process of evaporating, and I think that trend will continue.

A second consequence would be that national savings would fall far short of what is needed to provide for investment and economic growth. The deficit devours about half of the total amount of this country's savings. That means the United States is going to grow only half as fast as it would have grown or else it will have to continue borrowing from overseas and selling its capital stock to foreigners. The United States is putting itself in the same position that Latin American countries have been in during our lifetime and the same position that Britain was in during the 1960s. In other words, we will have some headaches.

COMMENT: I assume you are talking about inflation.

MR. McKINNEY: Inflation may be among our headaches, but not necessarily. A deficit is going to add marbles to the bowl, and if the Federal Reserve does what the American people hired them to do, they will take marbles out of the bowl. We might well be able to get by without inflation coming to fruition, but that would be because the Fed was exerting superhuman efforts, not because of fiscal policy.

QUESTION: I see the public resisting your remedies on two grounds. First, many Americans perceive themselves as getting poorer, and therefore, unable to afford a tax increase. Second, many people would consider it unfair to raise the payroll tax. How would you address these concerns?

MR. McKINNEY: The notion that Americans cannot afford a tax increase is absolutely wrong. Taxes are a form of national saving and we are short on national saving. We are overspending our incomes, so we need more national saving. One way to accomplish that would be to increase taxes, which would strengthen our productive machinery and make for a faster real growth rate. We and our children would be better off if we had the tax increase, if that were the only way of getting a budget closer into balance.

How would fairness in any tax increase be preserved? My personal conception of a fair tax system is one that preserves the optimal relationship between individual people's desire to improve their own circumstances by saving and working on one hand, and society's desire to have the opportunity to increase their well-being at the fastest rate—that is, a balanced system. A balanced system in my mind is one that has a progressive tax *system*. That is not the same thing as whether one piece of the system is progressive.

People make the mistake of looking at one tax as if it represented the *whole* objective. It does not. We should try to maintain a tax system where the total of all the taxes is reasonably progressive, yet offers maximum opportunities for everyone all the way up the ladder. There is plenty of room for argument as to which tax should be increased. Personally, I would increase income taxes first, simply because it is easier to administer than some of the others, but I would also look at alternative potential tax revenue sources.

QUESTION: The balanced-budget amendment is a big political issue. Do the proponents of this amendment intend to eliminate cyclical as well as structural deficits?

MR. McKINNEY: As the amendment is generally presented, it would eliminate cyclical deficits and therefore would be unequivocally bad if it were put through in its current form. A second problem I have with the balanced-budget amendment is that it is another bit of posturing that deceives people into believing the Congress is going to do something when they aren't.

Why should we monkey around with that grand old document called the Constitution and demand that Congress balance the budget when there is already a balanced-budget requirement in the Constitution? There is no point in passing another one. The Constitution gives Congress the sole power to tax and spend and the sole power to borrow money. Every year they must pass a borrowing resolution that authorizes the national debt limit to be increased or left where it was. How much closer can you come to having a balanced-budget amendment? As it stands now, an affirmative vote of Congress is required to permit an unbalanced budget. I would strongly oppose the balanced-budget amendment because I think it is pure fraud.

QUESTION: I take it then that your first choice is to reduce spending, but you do not think Congress and the President will get together in doing so. If Congress passes the budget cuts proposed by the Republicans, would that change your mind?

MR. McKINNEY: A great deal of fraud and hypocrisy can go on between now and five to ten years in the future. Instead of passing a long-term, budget-balancing resolution, I would much rather see Congress aiming to balance the budget this year, next year, and the year after.

COMMENT: I am concerned about how close our country is to political and financial ruin.

MR. McKINNEY: The country is not close to that condition yet; it is only at the stage of having to take a backseat role in multilateral policy decisions. France continues to tell us where to go on military matters, and the "tigers" in the Pacific Rim tell us where to go on economic matters. Our presidents talk about foreign policy matters but the United States does not have the muscle to carry them out. Erosion of global influence doesn't happen overnight, but it does happen. Domestically, a slower rate of economic growth will leave our children with a weaker and less viable economy than they would otherwise have had.

QUESTION: You want to balance the federal budget by cutting spending. Let's say for the sake of argument that everyone takes a hit—defense, Medicare, and so forth. What percentage of the programs would have to be cut in order to balance the budget?

MR. McKINNEY: The total federal budget this year is close to $1.5 trillion and our deficit is running about $200 billion, maybe 2 or 3 percent of gross national product. Programs could take that kind of cut without worrying about it too much, as long as it were made across-the-board.

QUESTION: Would you comment on the difficulty of reconciling political reality with economic reality?

MR. McKINNEY: That is the key question, I guess. How can we get meaningful cuts in government spending when Senator Dole backs off from reducing agricultural subsidy payments at the very beginning of the debate over how to cut the deficit? How do we get around congressmen from California and Texas who do everything they can to make sure their particular spending programs remain intact? Who has been proposing that the peanut quota or tobacco quota be cut? Not very many people here in Virginia.

A number of years ago, Phil Gramm figured out the ratio between the number of people who have an interest in a particular spending cut and the number of people who have an interest in it not being cut. The typical beneficiary of a government spending program gets approximately $500 from it. (I don't remember the exact figure but I do remember the ratio.) American people in general contribute $5 toward that $500. With comparatively so little at stake, they don't bother to go down to Washington and complain to their congressmen about, say, government price supports for sugar beet farmers in the far West. The guys who receive the $500 are the ones who go down to Washington and lobby their congressmen and senators. The moral is that a democracy may not be the best way to run an efficient economy.

During the 1960s, for example, governmental advisers tried to stimulate economic activity beyond the rate of growth at which it could be sustained over the long run, thereby leading to the sharp inflation of the 1970s that set this country up for what has been happening ever since. To understand the origins of the predicament we are in, one must go back to at least the early 1960s to find the major economic mistakes that were perpetuated by politicians and supported by the American people. I don't know how to get around that problem.

COMMENT: Can you imagine a political candidate running on the platform of trimming Social Security and reducing Medicare being elected?

MR. McKINNEY: That is a good point. A recent poll found that more than 80 percent of the American people do not want Social Security and Medicare programs to be trimmed in order to balance the budget. Over 70 percent, I believe it was, do not want the Medicaid program trimmed in order to balance the budget. That suggests there is strong popular support for leaving those outlays where they are. As a practical matter, if the amount of cutting done from the discretionary end of the budget is totaled, there is not much left. Social Security accounts for about 22 percent of the total, Medicare and Medicaid account for another 19 percent, and if interest on the federal budget deficit is included, the figure is about 54 percent of the total budget. If military spending is included, the total rises to 72 percent of the budget. Either some pretty big cuts must be made in that 72 percent area or the objectives will not be accomplished. I agree that trying to convince voters of the necessity of doing so is a problem.

QUESTION: I agree with your argument that cyclical deficits can serve a useful purpose. When you talk about balancing the budget a few years from now, shouldn't you be talking about balancing the structural deficit rather than the cyclical deficit?

MR. McKINNEY: I say "balancing the budget" as a shortcut; what I mean is substantially balancing the structural budget, not the cyclical budget. Actually, there is not much problem with the cyclical budget deficit because whenever we move into a recession, public opinion and congressional opinion generally shift in favor of taking corrective measures. People should not object to those measures or the built-in automatic stabilizers. Nevertheless, they *should* object when 3 percent structural deficits are allowed to persist year after year, decade after decade.

QUESTION: So theoretically, a $40 billion deficit a few years from now might not be a bad idea?

MR. McKINNEY: It depends on the state of the economy at the time. If a deficit occurs when we are at substantially full employment, I certainly would object. That would be a structural deficit.

QUESTION: Assuming the budget is balanced, will the debt ever be repaid?

MR. McKINNEY: I certainly hope not! Eddie Wayne, the former president of the Richmond Federal Reserve Bank, used to say that after you run over a person going one way with an inflationary debt increase, it doesn't make much sense to run over him again going back the other way. I think that is exactly what would be involved in paying off the national debt. The proper economic analysis, I think, hinges not on the absolute size of the debt, although there are related peripheral issues. Basically, we are talking about this year's *increase* in the debt, or this year's budget deficit. An economy cannot live without credit, and the other side of the credit coin is debt. Let's not try to pay off the national debt.

QUESTION: How does one counter the argument that since the government has neither a capital budget nor a set of depreciation accounts, the 3 percent deficit, which corresponds approximately to the value of the capital purchases of the government, should therefore be excluded from the structural deficit?

MR. McKINNEY: That is a legitimate point, but it has something to do with your view of what the role of the government ought to be and what degree of socialization of the economy that you believe is appropriate. If you are talking about what is already being done in the way of infrastructure and capital investment, that is one of the good arguments the technicians ought to use in deciding how big the deficit ought to be. I would grant you the implied point that *some* capital investments by the government yield productive benefits in the future. Nevertheless, I still think our nation is growing too slowly and that the potential savings diverted into overseas purchases because of the budget deficit *does* tend to cause some serious problems.

NARRATOR: Thank your for your well-prepared presentation concerning serious policy questions. We are grateful to you for an excellent Forum.

« CHAPTER 6 »

THE BUDGET PROCESS[*]

BRYCE L. HARLOW

NARRATOR: Larry Harlow is vice president and director of legislative affairs for Timmons and Company, Inc., one of the premier government relations consulting firms in Washington. Before joining Timmons and Company, Inc., in 1991, he served for a decade in six senior federal government positions for the Reagan and Bush administrations.

Before working with the Reagan administration, Mr. Harlow directed a governmental relations program for a major trade association in Washington, D.C., and previous to that position, he handled relations with six state legislatures in the Rocky Mountain region for the U.S. Environmental Protection Agency. He also worked in the United States Senate as an aide to one of our Council members, Senator Howard H. Baker.

At the beginning of the Reagan administration Mr. Harlow served as director of the Office of Legislation at the Environmental Protection Agency. Late in 1981 with the confirmation of a new chairman at the Federal Trade Commission, he joined that group and established the first free-standing Office of Congressional Relations in that organization. In the second Reagan term he

---

*Presented in a Forum at the Miller Center of Public Affairs on 2 December 1994.

served as special assistant to the President for legislative affairs again and remained in the Executive Office of the President for President Reagan's entire second term.

At the beginning of the Bush administration, Larry Harlow was nominated by the President and confirmed by the Senate as assistant secretary of the treasury for legislative affairs.

I cannot forbear mentioning that perhaps the figure who gave us most heart when we began this oral history program was Larry Harlow's father, Bryce Harlow. Of all of the people who participated in and interpreted the presidency, he has been ranked by people of all political persuasions as the ablest and the most clearheaded. I had the privilege of interviewing Bryce Harlow at Harper's Ferry and Crystal City about his experience in the Nixon and Eisenhower administrations.

As for Larry Harlow, his record stands by itself and attests to his strengths and achievements. We are delighted that he could join us to speak about the Bush administration.

MR. HARLOW: I was puzzled by the invitation to speak at the Miller Center. I wondered what on earth a bureaucrat bent and bowed by ten years of service to two administrations could have to say that would be of interest. I realized, however, that I was part of the Bush administration during its first two years when the emphasis was on the budget and on which little has yet been said. Perhaps I can share some experiences from the perspective of someone who was in the trenches for ten years and who saw what went wrong in those first two years of the Bush administration. Those first two years defined the shortcomings of the administration over the entire four-year period.

I would like to step back to 1989 and remind you of the atmosphere that existed at the beginning of the Bush administration. The administration coming into office was to be a kinder, gentler administration. The President and Congress enjoyed their normal six-month honeymoon period. There was a tremendous budget problem, and one priority of the administration and budget officials of the executive branch was to do something about it.

President Bush, unlike President Reagan, was a creature of the legislature. He had served in the House and had spent a great deal of his career in Washington. Everyone in Washington expected that there would be a new atmosphere of give-and-take with the wheeling-and-dealing Democratic Congress and that the continued confrontations between Congress and the President that took place during the Reagan administration would subside. For that reason, a great deal of enthusiasm, optimism, and "we can do it" spirit could be found in Washington in early 1989—much as what one sees at the beginning of each administration, such as that of 1993. The new administration of 1989 was a little different, however, because of the seasoning of the individuals involved.

The President had wonderful relationships with Dan Rosten-kowski, one of his best friends and chairman of the Ways and Means Committee, and Tom Foley, the soon-to-be Speaker of the House. Jim Wright was still Speaker at the beginning of the administration. It seemed that the stars had aligned in the correct order so that something could be done once and for all about the budget deficit, which had been the subject by that point of three different so-called summits. Each summit was supposed to be the one that would solve the mess, but the deficit increased after each one because the spending continued.

Ironically, despite these factors, the administration decided at the beginning that the best approach would be to put off coming to final answers on the budget because any of the final answers would involve a repudiation of the campaign pledge "Read my lips, no new taxes." Any attempt to do something serious and final about the deficit would have had to include a sizeable revenue package because the Democrats clearly would have refused to approve the kind of significant budget process reform or entitlement reform necessary for lowering spending to a level where a sizeable deficit reduction over a long period of time could be achieved. Thus, the administration budget officials decided to begin 1989 with the small package. They decided to aim for the big package in 1990.

A problem occurred in 1989, however, when the small package became subsumed by the issue of capital gains, a debate that defined the nature of the relationship between the administration and Congress for the remainder of the Bush term. The Reconcilia-tion Bill resulting from the budget agreement of 1989 began to move through Congress, when it suddenly occurred to some of us at the Treasury Department that we probably had the votes in the Ways and Means Committee to pass one of the President's campaign pledges, a reduction of the capital gains tax. We decided to see if in fact that was the case, and after a week of work, we had enough votes in the Ways and Means Committee to pass the bill reducing the capital gains tax.

We were not able to work out a deal with the committee's chairman, however. The leader of the House of Representatives, Dick Gephardt, was unalterably opposed to it. We then discovered that George Mitchell, who was in his first term as leader of the Senate and who had been cooperative over the years with all of the Reagan and Bush administrations' previous budget reduction efforts, felt that he had been given a commitment from administration budget officials not to raise the issue in 1989. He thought that the administration had promised not to raise the issue until 1990. No one in the administration can remember making that commitment, and for various reasons, it was decided that the commitment did not exist. As a result, George Mitchell felt betrayed, and his sense of betrayal, founded or unfounded, poisoned the atmosphere from that point forward on any budget or domestic agenda issues that were at issue between the administration and the leader of the U.S. Senate.

A huge fight occurred over the proposed capital gains tax reduction, but it eventually passed in the House. It did not pass the Senate, however, despite the administration's parliamentary advantage against Mitchell in the Senate. The bill was Mitchell's first big test as majority leader. We planned to attach the bill to the debt limit extension so we would have leverage over him. We reasoned that Mitchell would feel pressure to grant the extension in a timely fashion because of the dramatic consequences if he did not. Mitchell, however, refused to allow us to bring it up. He begged the Republicans to back off in the name of good government, and he promised to vote for it later. Knowing that this was George Mitchell's first huge issue out of the box, Bob Dole decided to allow Mitchell some leeway and backed off on the issue. The high-water mark of the capital gains issue came when Dole gave Mitchell control of the floor. At that point George Mitchell found a way to forget his commitment to give Republicans the vote. When the vote finally occurred later in the year, Mitchell filibustered the Republicans. They needed 60 votes to win but only received 51 votes. That battle and the rancor accompanying it set the stage for the huge budget summit in 1990 and the distrust that permeated the process.

In 1989, with the Treasury Department running the legislative efforts, the administration had a wonderfully successful year. Except for the capital gains issue, we had replenished the savings and loans through the Congress and had resolved other budget issues; it seemed as though everything was set for the next year.

In 1990, administration officials tried to engage in summitry again with the leaders of Congress. At first, every member of Congress who was potentially interested in budget issues—and that meant every member of Congress—wanted to sit in on these meetings. As one can imagine, every one of these people wanted to have a say in the final outcome, which is a problem given that the goal of summitry is to reduce the number of participants. Large groups make it difficult to reach a solution to a problem. In 1990, the process began with a large group of participants.

To reduce the number of participants, one must prove that the big group is not efficient. For months, nothing but political posturing happened in these meetings. One side would make an inflammatory remark, and the other side would answer with another inflammatory remark, wink at each other, and return later to the meeting. The administration and Congress developed a tacit understanding that they would not make any progress. This understanding allowed Democratic leaders to get rid of those Democrats they did not want in the meetings and allowed the Republicans in the administration and the Republican leaders in Congress to winnow down the number of Republicans. In short, the reduction process worked, and the groups began to shrink. The problem was that they ultimately shrank too much. The group that finally cut the deal at the end of 1990 was too small. It no longer represented a majority of the rank and file in Congress.

From the administration's standpoint, the small groups posed a different problem. As soon as the groups became small enough for someone to suggest going to the Oval Office for discussions, the administration had a problem.

The administration's handling of the 1990 budget summit was characterized by a series of mistakes, one after another. The first mistake was in allowing any discussions to take place in the Oval Office. In essence, Dick Gephardt, George Mitchell, Leon Panetta (then the budget chairman in the House), and Jim Sasser (budget chairman in the Senate) were allowed to come into the Oval Office and sit down with Richard Darman, Nicholas Brady, John Sununu, and the President to discuss the budget. Once these men were allowed to negotiate in the Oval Office, the President was no longer in a position to disavow whatever was happening. When someone would say that they had heard talk about taxes, he is no longer in a position to say, "That was Brady. I didn't say it." Part of the job of a Cabinet official is to be there, frankly, to take the heat off the president. Once the president's advisers allow the president to be exposed, he can no longer disavow the outcome and thus would have a direct stake in the success of the process. In short, any failure of the process would be viewed as a failure for George Bush.

The other mistake, a huge tactical mistake that characterized the discussions in 1990, was the failure of administration officials to heed, stroke, caress, and keep the Republicans in Congress and across the country informed on what was happening. The best example of this was when administration officials failed to inform Republicans about the decision to renege on President Bush's "no new taxes" pledge. During a meeting in the Oval Office with Democratic leaders, President Bush decided to put out a statement that revenues would be negotiable and put on the table. Either John Sununu or Dick Darman wrote the statement and handed it to Gephardt, who then handed it to Mitchell, who then asked that some changes be made. I cannot recall if any Republican leaders were present at the meeting, but the statement was retyped to reflect the new wording. It was then given to Marlin Fitzwater with instructions to post it on the press bulletin board.

I know this story intimately because of my own involvement. I happened to be in the Senate press gallery at the time, and I noticed that people were suddenly beginning to move around with alacrity and excitement. My pager went off, and I returned a call to the chief of staff for the secretary of the treasury. He said, "I just learned that a statement was put on the press board in the

White House about ten minutes ago. Let me read it to you."
Included in this statement was the phrase, "including new revenues"
to be put on the table. I said, "There goes the pledge! There goes
'no new taxes'!" I told him I would get back to him and then called
Fred McClure, the head of White House legislative affairs. I asked
McClure if he knew about the statement, and he indicated that he
did not. I then read him the portion that I had written down, and
he said, "Talk to you later." I then called David Demarest, who
was in charge of Public Liaison operations, and told him about the
statement. Both he and McClure ran to the press room, fought
through the reporters, and read the statement. They were immediately aghast and ran back to their offices and madly began making
calls in an attempt to get ahead of the curve, but they were of
course unable to do so.

At that point, Republicans on the Hill were being confronted
by reporters, saying, "What do you think of this statement?" "What
statement?" they asked. "The statement about the taxes that will
be on the table. Did they check with you before they put this out?"
"No," they answered, and doors were slamming and papers flying.
The Democrats, of course, were leaning back in their offices
yukking it up at that point, thinking, "Boy, we got them!"

The President was very poorly served that day. When President Bush indicated that he would approve the statement, someone
in that room—and that includes my boss, Nick Brady, for whom I
have enormous affection and respect, Dick Darman, and John
Sununu—should have said, "Mr. President, can I see you alone for
a second in the study?" They should have said to him, "We cannot
put this out without giving our guys a heads-up so they can cover
their tail ends. Give us half an hour." George Bush would have
realized they were right and given them a day to review the
statement. The alternative was to let Republican party faithfuls
around the country feel terribly betrayed by the President's not
telling them of this statement. As a result, those Republicans
walked away from the President and stayed away.

There is no question that this action had to be taken to get the
needed budget deficit reduction. The budget deficit needed to be
reduced to drive down interest rates around the world. The United
States had to demonstrate to world leaders and its own market that

it was serious about deficit reductions so that world leaders would take steps to stabilize interest rates. Moreover, the administration had every reason to believe that the Federal Reserve, upon seeing a sizeable deficit reduction, would lower interest rates in this country. Thus, there were many reasons for the President's decision.

We expected that this concession by the President would make budget negotiations go much more quickly and easily. That did not happen. The Democrats dragged their feet on everything they could throughout the summer. I don't fault the Democrats for this because we let them play this political game every step of the way. The decadent experience at Andrews Air Force Base followed. All of the officers were moved out of their officers' club, and the members of Congress and administration officials moved in. A ten-day discussion resulted in nothing but an agreement to shrink the group more, so the group shrank and went to Tom Foley's office. The group ultimately went to Mitchell's office and all over the Capitol trying to come up with a final agreement.

Before the meetings at Andrews began, Newt Gingrich had already begun to send signals to the White House saying, "You guys had better be careful; the troops are restless; they've never gotten over this 'no new taxes' thing." Gingrich began to show signs that he was not comfortable with what was occurring, especially after the group shrank more. Note what is happening here: Newt Gingrich, the leader of the Republican conservatives in the House of Representatives, was no longer a participant in the negotiations. Though it might have bothered those already in the room, further negotiations should not have proceeded without Gingrich because he was the one who controlled a sizeable block of votes. This litany of tactical mistakes is edifying because it explains why we got into the mess we did.

The next mistake, which was related to the problem of excluding Newt Gingrich, occurred at the conference held by Republicans to talk about the deal that had been reached. At this conference one administration official told all of the Republicans in attendance—that is, every Republican member in the House of Representatives—that the President would be appearing in every congressional district across the country. The official said, "He will be in your district! He will stand on the platform in your district and ask you how you voted on the budget package." Carl Purcell, one of the President's best friends on the Hill, responded, "I have known George Bush longer than you have, and I can tell you right now that he would never go to a district and threaten another Republican with a comment like that." The administration official answered, "Maybe he won't, but I will." Brady and I were sitting there, appalled. Then another administration official got up and answered another member's question about public highway funding by saying, "Obviously, you are unable to understand this matter. Either that, or you don't listen—one of the two." Republican congressmen began shaking their heads and leaving the room. Obviously, the administration was in trouble at this point with respect to getting the necessary number of votes.

It did not need to be that way. Most of those who attended the conference wanted to help George Bush because, frankly, helping George Bush would have helped them. Instead, they came out of the meeting so aggravated and offended by what they thought was the arrogant behavior of the administration that when the vote came up, the Republicans lost, mainly because of the defection of Republican conservatives. They rejected the package in large part to send a signal, not a very pleasant one, to the administration. By voting down the bill, however, the Republicans created a situation in which the administration had to fashion a package to attract more Democratic votes. Thus from the Republican perspective, the package became worse. They knew what was going to happen, but they defeated the bill in part because they were fed up with the way they were being treated by the administration.

This example shows how much of everything going on in Washington is determined by the kinds of human relationships, friendships, and basic rules and protocols that govern day-to-day behavior between humans in every type of relationship across the country.

The bottom line is that the administration became untrustworthy in the eyes of the Republicans on the Hill whose votes we needed. That distrust itself was a result of a number of tactical missteps by the administration during this time. Through their behavior, congressional Republicans communicated their distrust of the administration to the voters, so that the Republican faithful lost their trust in the President too. President Bush was never able to recover this trust even after the Gulf War. As a result, Bill Clinton was elected.

Bill Clinton is now having the same problem. He has lost the trust of the American people. Once you lose that trust, you don't get it back.

QUESTION: Where was the President when all of this was building up? Was he aware of what was happening and did he keep a hand on it?

MR. HARLOW: Yes, to a certain extent. George Bush's focus was not domestic politics. He had very capable budget officials. For example, Richard Darman is one of the smartest people I have ever met. He certainly was capable of handling all of these issues from the spending side. Nick Brady was highly respected on Capitol Hill; those on the Hill trusted him, and I want to emphasize that fact. Darman may have all of the facts and figures, but Brady had the character they respected. When the deal was going to be cut, they wanted Nick Brady in the room. They knew that if he sat there and nodded, he was reflecting the President's position.

The President was brought up-to-date weekly, or even daily, when things got down to the crunch. The White House normally has weekly legislative leadership meetings in the White House. I don't know if such meetings have occurred as frequently in the Clinton administration, but the Reagan and Bush administrations, as well as the Nixon, Eisenhower, and Ford administrations, held weekly meetings with congressional leaders—either Republican leaders or a bipartisan group of leaders. Obviously, budget issues were always discussed. President Bush had an ability to grasp these things quickly, to understand the basics, and to argue and articulate the issues. He was directly involved in trying to get the budget passed. The problem is that once the president is pulled into this process, as Bush was, his prestige becomes dependent on the outcome. It becomes his loss; it becomes his budget. Bush raised the members of Congress up to his level when he let them into the Oval Office. It is all right to bring them into the Cabinet room for the weekly leadership meetings, but to have them in the Oval Office negotiating the budget is a mistake because it puts the president himself at risk. One wants the secretary of the treasury or the director of OMB to be at risk, but not the president.

QUESTION: How do you feel about tampering with the capital gains tax, both in terms of the importance that was placed on it and in terms of the wisdom of it?

MR. HARLOW: In terms of doing it, I strongly favor a reduction in the capital gains tax—a 50 percent exclusion, such as what we are talking about now. It would unlock resources that have been locked up by people not wanting to pay the tax. The situation is already better now than it was in the period I have just discussed because there is now a 28 percent cap on the capital gains tax. In essence, they lowered the cap by raising all other tax rates. As a result, it is advantageous at the present time for investors to unlock their gains and reinvest them because they only pay a 28 percent tax. The Republicans in general, certainly the House Republicans and most Senate Republicans, continue to feel that further reducing that rate to exclude half of capital gains income would further stimulate the economy by encouraging people to cash in and reinvest.

In terms of the importance placed on it, I thought far too much had been placed on it. It should not become the mantra for the Republican party. As I said before, Republicans won a great victory in the House of Representatives on capital gains, and they had the Democrats in a box in the Senate. They could have made Mitchell and his colleagues blink. All they wanted was an up or down vote on capital gains. The Democrats were filibustering against them, making them come up with 60 votes. Once Republicans succumbed to George Mitchell's good-government argument and backed off on the debt-limit bill, however, Mitchell did exactly what he had been accusing Republicans of doing. As a result, the Republicans could not come up with the necessary 60 votes. When Republicans finally had their vote on capital gains, they only received 51 votes. That is nine votes short of what they needed. Republicans would have had the votes to pass capital gains if it had been a normal vote, not a cloture vote.

I do not think the capital gains issue is the be-all and end-all, frankly. It should not define the Republican party. Nevertheless, at this point, it is unavoidable and will be a key part of the package that comes out of the House and the first one on the desk, if it—again—can get through the Senate.

QUESTION: The Federal Reserve has been increasing interest rates, presumably in an effort to control the expansion of certain resources that would follow an increased reduction in the capital gains tax. Should the Federal Reserve be increasing interest rates?

MR. HARLOW: The Federal Reserve does not need to increase interest rates any more.

QUESTION: Is it acceptable to allow expansion to continue uncontrolled?

MR. HARLOW: Yes, expansion should be permitted to continue. I am not an economist, and I am not going to pretend to be one. I do have certain views on the matter, however, based on my experience heading OMB legislative affairs and Treasury Department legislative affairs and my involvement in many of these issues in the White House, however. I think what the Fed has done is good for the long-term health of the economy, but enough is enough. I think the expansion should be allowed to grow more than it has and that unlocking these resources—these capital gains—for reinvestment in long-term investments is, again, good for the country. I would like to see people free their capital gains and reinvest them in other long-term investments in the country. I am not talking about freeing the capital gains so people will run out and spend them. I do not think people would do that. They will find other ways to invest them, perhaps in new types of investments or new types of growth investment in the country. This will serve the country's best interests in the long term. I do not have hard empirical data with me to back up my statements, but that is what I think will happen.

QUESTION: What do you foresee for the Gingrich-Archer formulated budget and its passage?

MR. HARLOW: They are in desperate shape, frankly. Right now, pandemonium reigns behind closed doors in Washington, and I have to race back to be trampled by it this afternoon. The Republicans now are like the dog that caught the car, particularly in the budget sense. Remember, the House Republicans have never been responsible for preparing a House budget resolution because they have never had control of the House since the establishment of that process. The Senate Republicans are in slightly better condition because Pete Domenici has done it before. They have been responsible for Senate budget resolutions, but they have never been responsible for one in conjunction with the House.

In the budget process, the president submits a budget. It is then immediately discarded, and the House and the Senate each write their own budget. They come together, and a conference committee writes a congressional budget resolution that is the budget of the United States of America. That version will include the so-called reconciliation instructions, which will include spending cuts and tax increases reconciled to the various committees of Congress and the various subject areas. The Republican staff in the House right now is just a shadow of the staff that the Democrats have had for years. I'm not saying this as a partisan. I think any objective observer would look at the way the staffs have been treated in the House of Representatives, particularly over the last 15 to 20 years, and see it as a travesty of justice and probably a usurpation of representative democracy. For instance, on Energy and Commerce, there are 140 Democratic staff members and 17 Republicans. How is that reflective of the 62 percent Democrat majority in the House of Representatives? It isn't! As a result of these staff imbalances that have built up over a long period of time, one Republican staffer was trying to do what five or six would be doing on the Democrat side. It is remarkable that the Republican staffers have done as good a job as they have.

The result is that now the Republican have control, they are incredibly unprepared because they have been browbeaten and hammered down for the last 20 years. Because the new Congress does not come in until January, that same small Republican staff is trying to develop a budget that was supposed to have been started in August. When the six Republicans on the House Budget Committee suddenly found themselves in charge of the process, they thought, "Maybe we had better call the Commerce and Treasury departments and find out what they want." To their surprise, they found that the Treasury Department and the Commerce Department are run by Democrats who do not feel like cooperating one bit with the Republicans.

The Republicans are in a difficult situation because of procedural problems that they face and because there is not enough money to do what they want to do. So Newt Gingrich makes comments like, "Let's put Social Security off budget." Budget officials hear that and have to be helped off the floor because if Social Security is put off budget, about a quarter or a third of the federal revenues would be wiped out, which would be disastrous. That is what they are going through. Archer will be able to move quickly in some areas and not so quickly in others.

Other factors are at work here as well. The Republicans in the House of Representatives have made a commitment to have a so-called open house. Thus, 75 percent of the bills to be considered on the House floor will be considered under a so-called open rule. That practice used to be the norm in the House of Representatives but was abandoned during the tenure of Tip O'Neill and Jim Wright, so that almost everything that came to the floor in the House was written with precise rules by the Democrats to keep Republicans from being able to offer amendments on certain subjects. In short, the Democrats controlled the entire process.

Republicans have said that this approach is wrong and that they will do something about it. They intend to live up to their promise. Now when bills come to the floor, people can come up with many ways to amend them. That has happened for some time in the Senate, which does not have germaneness rules. Senators can add an amendment on any topic to a bill. The Senate process is based on unanimous consent so agreement is necessary for everything. It has not always happened that way in the House, however. Think about that when a capital gains bill moves to the floor. Democrats will be able to come in from left field and get amendments included on all types of other controversial issues with only the flimsiest thread of germaneness. The new open-house rule will make it very difficult for the Republicans to live up to their pledge of passing bills in the first 100 days of the new Congress.

What people will probably see is Newt Gingrich having absolute control over the Republicans in the House, where they will back him on every parliamentary ruling from the chair. He will have to have that kind of control or there will be pandemonium on the House floor because the Democrats will jump up and do whatever they want and try to embarrass the Republicans and have a good old time on C-SPAN. The parliamentarian or Gingrich will make rulings from the chair. They will try to be concise with them, but sometimes they will be provocative and controversial. When that happens, the Democrats will appeal the ruling of the chair, and it will come down to the majority ruling. Rules are only good as long as votes are available to back them up. Rules votes will take up a great deal of time on the House floor because of these types of problems.

No one part of the Republican pledge can be looked at alone. There will be a domino effect. Dominoes could be stretched from here to Washington that have to be tipped over regarding the changes now occurring in that town.

QUESTION: What do you think about the chances of cutting government—for example, by reducing the sizes of staffs and committees?

MR. HARLOW: The chances are very good. There will be a reduction in the size of staff in the House of Representatives. The committee staffs will be reduced by one-third, and there will be fewer committees. There will have to be fewer committees because one of the rule changes the Republicans will make is to end the practice of proxy voting, where an absentee committee member gives the chairman or someone else a proxy, and that person votes it the way he or she wants. Republicans are going to stop that practice because it has led to the proliferation of committees and subcommittees. Requiring the presence of committee members to vote would limit the number of committees on which a single representative could serve because he or she can only be in one place at a time. Thus, the elimination of proxy voting will necessarily shrink the number of committees in the House.

It will also shrink the size of committees. Committees have become huge. The Appropriations Committee in the House now has 62 members, but it will soon shrink to about 52 members once proxy voting is eliminated.

The Republicans will not do anything as dramatic as the things they maintained immediately after the election. They will not eliminate the Energy and Commerce Committee, for instance. They will do some fine-tuning. The Republican strategy is based upon the thesis that real changes can only be made right after an election that has changed control of Congress and before the new party is in power. Otherwise, the vested interests and the bureaucracies link up with their appropriate committees, and the iron triangle is back in place. The members on the committees do not want to give up their relationships to the bureaucracies or to the vested interests that are now special interests that have become beholden to them.

NARRATOR: Could you refresh everyone's minds about iron triangles?

MR. HARLOW: The reference I used for iron triangles—and there are others—is the relationship between a powerful committee in Congress, the bureaucracy that is beholden to that committee, and the special interests regulated by the bureaucracy that try to influence the committee that writes the laws regulating the bureaucracy. The committees are responsive to the constituencies because the constituencies help committee members get elected; thus it is a representative democracy in that sense. Once iron triangles are in place, it is extremely difficult to break them up.

QUESTION: With respect to Bush's unexpected decision to make revenues negotiable, you mentioned that a half hour's or day's warning might have allowed the administration's spokesmen or spinners to make the decision palatable to other Republicans. Would you comment further on this issue?

MR. HARLOW: Ideally, this development would have occurred over a period of months, during which the administration would have successfully demonstrated its commitment to deficit reductions by its many concrete spending cut proposals and other revenue-raising ideas—such as user fees, which were rejected by the Democrats. The administration had made such proposals, but the public was not aware of them. Everything happened behind closed doors.

One of the lessons to Republicans of this process is that such closed-door methods are not in their interest. In 1990, the budget negotiations were moved to Andrews Air Force Base to cloak them in secrecy and to keep any knowledge of the negotiations from becoming public so that we could work in a trustful atmosphere. The Democrats, of course, leaked a great deal of information. I am not saying this as a partisan, but the next day we could read in the newspaper what had been said the day before. Republicans were playing by the rules and not talking to the media. Members of the media today tell me, "You guys were being played; you were such idiots. Every day after the negotiations, people for Mitchell and Sasser on the Budget Committee would brief us and put their spin on what was taking place. You guys didn't do a thing, did you?" We replied that we thought we were playing by the rules. They called us babes in the woods! We should have played the game and set the situation up much better than we did.

In August of 1989, about four of us went to Easton, Maryland, to sit down with Secretary Brady in the basement of an old home of his and review the situation. We concluded that given the need to send a message to the markets and do something about international interest rates we needed a budget deal, and we would have to put revenues on the table if we wanted a budget deal. There was no way around it.

Once that decision was made, two questions remained: When should we do it, and How should we do it? With respect to the first question of timing, we wanted to do it as far in front of the next election as possible. To do it immediately before the next election would have been self-immolation. We thought it would be wise to put revenues on the table as quickly as possible. I think the timing issue was properly decided. It was the second question of how to do it that was botched.

The failure to handle this issue properly is an indication of what was structurally wrong inside the White House. To put it bluntly, everything was at the top, and not enough bait was put in the White House apparatus to convince people to do the job they had been hired to do. The administration should have had Demarest handle public relations with its constituencies and Fred McClure handle the Congress, but that was not done. If it had been handled in that manner, the umbrage and feeling of betrayal might have been greatly diminished. In answer to your question then, all of the blame cannot be laid on that one instant, but this episode is a great example and probably the crowning moment of our tactical mismanagement of the entire 1990 budget process.

NARRATOR: Other presidents have put foreign policy first. For example, Nixon chose his foreign policy team before he did anything else, and people are still puzzled that his domestic and economic team was as weak as it was. In the Bush administration, some people have said that Nick Brady lacked the necessary knowledge for the position he held. Was the media attention focused on Brady and the others one reason the economic policy suffered?

MR. HARLOW: There was a conscious decision in the administration to resolve what it saw as the outstanding domestic issues in the first two years before turning to foreign policy in the second two years. The situation in Kuwait changed that to a certain degree. Iraq's invasion of Kuwait took place in August 1990, just before we went into the summit conference at Andrews Air Force Base. Incidentally, Brady joined the budget summit conference at Andrews straight off a plane on which he had flown around the world raising money from the allies for the war effort. Though successful, Brady came into the budget summit without any sleep, exhausted.

To be fair in assessing the administration's handling of the budget process, people should consider that the President was in a box once Kuwait occurred. If the budget process did not reach a successful conclusion, a sequester of incredible proportions would have resulted. This sequester would have sent a terrible message to our putative allies about our commitment in this area and about our ability to get our act together. Once the United States was headed toward war with Iraq—actually, once the United States even began efforts to get Saddam Hussein out of Kuwait—we could not allow the message to be sent that the United States was going to cut defense forces by one-third. The sequester would have been of monumental proportions. For instance, the United States might not have had the ability to airlift troops and supplies on a moment's notice. Finishing the budget quickly became a priority. The necessity for haste has to be factored into any analysis of the budget situation.

Regarding your point about domestic versus foreign policy, remember that Nixon was successful domestically during the first two years of his administration. He was very successful in creating the Environmental Protection Agency and various other domestic initiatives. He had problems, obviously, with some Supreme Court nominations, as George Bush did with John Tower's nomination as secretary of defense, but by and large Nixon was in a strong position. George Bush was not necessarily in a strong position heading into the last two years of his term. His weakened position is a reflection of the problems the United States had domestically those first two years. The first year was very successful, but the second year was a disaster.

QUESTION: If Newt Gingrich appoints the chairmen of those various committees, will he be overreaching his power or authority? Will he create disharmony in the Republican party as a result?

MR. HARLOW: The Speaker of the House is elected by members of the majority party. If he is overreaching himself, they will not elect him as Speaker. It is important to remember that over half of the Republican party in the House of Representatives are either freshmen or just finishing their first terms and beginning their second terms. Thus, over half of the Republican members are newcomers. As a bloc, they are the ones that have the votes on Newt Gingrich. Gingrich has to be responsive to these new people. My friend who is participating in the transition meetings said, "I'm going into these meetings all the time with these little kids, and then I realize they are congressmen!" That is what Gingrich is dealing with.

I think Gingrich will be elected by acclamation. He is considered the prophet by Republicans in the House. He was the only one who believed the Republicans could win a majority.

Last night I was with Newt at a dinner where he gave an extemporaneous speech, which is the way he delivers all of his speeches. He does not use notes or read from text. Gingrich is very intelligent, and he retains everything. He is doing a great job of handling this transition. The proof will be seen on opening day. The House will have the longest opening day in the history of the Republic. It will enact all of the rule changes Republicans promised. On that day, Congress will pass legislation to guarantee an open House and a reduction in the size of its committees. It will mark a dramatic change in the operations of the House. I think as time passes, the American people will like Newt Gingrich more and more. Frankly, I am making comments that I would not have made four years ago about Newt Gingrich, but I am completely sold on him now. He has done a fabulous job, and he is doing a better job every day in the way he is handling himself.

NARRATOR: We have been very fortunate to have Larry Harlow with us today. He knows government well and has made a significant contribution to our Bush oral history series.

III

THE ECONOMICS AND POLITICS
OF THE DEBT AND THE DEFICIT

« CHAPTER 7 »

THE FEDERAL BUDGET DEFICIT
AND THE NATIONAL DEBT*

WILLIAM E. FRENZEL

NARRATOR: William Frenzel, a respected congressman serving his Minnesota constituency for 20 years, was equally respected on both sides of the aisle. He was ranking Minority member on the House Budget Committee and the principal Republican economic spokesman in the House of Representatives. He was also a member of the House Ways and Means Committee and a congressional representative to the General Agreement on Tariffs and Trade (GATT) in Geneva for 15 years. In 1993 Mr. Frenzel was appointed special adviser to the President for the North American Free Trade Agreement (NAFTA). He also served as special adviser in 1994 to the National Association of Manufacturers for the GATT-Uruguay Round.

Mr. Frenzel received his bachelor's and master's degrees from Dartmouth College. During the Korean War, he served as a naval officer. He was a member of the Minnesota legislature for eight years and president of the Minneapolis Terminal Warehouse Company. He is currently serving as president of the Ripon Society and is a Distinguished Fellow of the Tax Foundation. He is also

*Presented in a Forum at the Miller Center of Public Affairs on 14 September 1995.

chairman of the Japan-America Society of Washington, chairman of the U.S. Steering Committee of the Transatlantic Policy Network, and vice chairman of the Eurasia Foundation. He has contributed to the U.S. national interest in many additional ways.

Bill Frenzel helped the Miller Center a great deal in its early history by serving as a member of the Miller Center commission on the presidential nominating process. We are honored to have him with us and grateful for his friendship in the past.

MR. FRENZEL: The budget deficit and the national debt are subjects that I delight in discussing because they are so important. People in Washington and elsewhere dread the "D" words. They make strong men tremble, women sob, and small children cry because it seems as though our nation will never get past them. I will first comment on where the United States stands regarding the deficit and who is responsible for the position in which this country finds itself. I will then discuss why the deficit was tolerated for so long by these perpetrators and conclude with a look to the future. Will history endlessly repeat itself, or is there hope for the future? I perceive there to be a small window of opportunity that may remain open for the next 60 days or so.

I slaved away in Congress for 20 years without making any apparent dent in the deficit. Despite my stern warnings to my colleagues about what awful things were going to happen if we did not deal with the deficit, the problem continued. The last budget of the United States written in black ink was for fiscal year 1969, more than 25 years ago. Thereafter, the rivers of red ink flowed. In fiscal year 1982 under President Reagan, the deficit reached the unprecedented level of over $100 billion. Since that year, the deficit has averaged higher than $200 billion annually. Over the last 23 years, the deficit has averaged about 4 percent of gross domestic product. The debt now owed by the United States is $4.9 trillion. If that figure were divided equally among the 250 million Americans, each one of us would owe approximately $20,000, and the tally grows higher every day.

Since most people have at least an idea that the deficit is unwise and that the debt is too big, it is clear that the Congress of the United States is the real villain. At the Founding, Americans had a great dislike for the Parliament of England, but they saved their strongest hate for King George III. When they formed the government, they decided that the people's representatives in the legislative branch should have the lion's share of the powers, particularly over raising and spending the people's money. Therefore they gave control of the purse to Congress. While many people say that the Framers created a balanced system of government in which the branches play off against each other with relatively equal powers, it has become clear to me, if not to other scholars, that the Congress has almost complete control over taxing and spending.

Over the years, the legislative branch has defended that power very aggressively; presidents were never able to intrude very far into the fiscal game except in time of dire emergency, such as depression or war. In fact, in the early 1970s Congress was willing to go to court to defeat the power of impoundment that presidents had exercised since 1803. In the *Chada* decision, the Supreme Court removed the power of impoundment from the president. This decision was later codified into law in the Budget Act of 1974, which meant that presidents could no longer impound monies that had been appropriated by Congress.

Whenever the Congress has been asked to cede other grants of fiscal power, such as the line-item veto, it has always said no. Instead, it has given the president a limited power of rescission; that is, the president can ask Congress to rescind a particular appropriation that he believes is unnecessary. Congress, however, does not even have to vote on whether to consider the rescission or not. It can simply ignore it. Over the years, Congress has accepted many rescissions that the president has proposed, but in terms of dollar amounts, they account for only a minuscule portion of the amount suggested. Thus, while the president has the ability to invoke rescission by law, it does not give him much real power.

The only real power the president has is the veto, which the Framers gave to him in the Constitution. The veto is a powerful weapon during budget negotiations because it is often used to persuade Congress to make changes in its appropriations bills. Once cast, however, the veto does not look nearly as strong. Although it can be overridden, Congress will more often bring up another bill that is a few dollars more or less than the one that was

127

vetoed, and then it is ultimately passed. The moment it is cast, the veto power begins to erode in strength, which continues until Congress passes the next bill.

The president, though, is not totally unarmed in his fiscal war with Congress. In fact, his strongest power may be what people call "moral suasion." The president from his bully pulpit can try to convince the public of the need to spend more money on certain programs or of the need to cut deficits. In my judgment, that power is probably more important than the veto. Even though it is not hard to identify the villain in this drama—I would say that about two-thirds of the blame for the deficits lies with Congress—the best efforts of both Congress and the president are required if anything is going to be accomplished.

Why would an otherwise sensible Congress get into this difficult position on deficits? What makes them so inefficient when handling money? Members of Congress appear to be sane when people meet them on the street, but fiscal policy in Congress does not follow rational patterns. It is not results-driven or process-driven. It is incentive-driven. These incentives have been with us since the 1930s when they were articulated in the Rooseveltian manner, "spend and elect." Members of Congress have seen over the years that if the government spends money on their individual consti-tuencies—whether the funds are targeted to benefit the elderly, agricultural interests, defense, highway promoters, universities, labor, environmentalists, techies, or whatever the cause may be—they invariably win reelection to Congress. Congress thus strives to reward the proper constituencies in the right sequences and amounts. During the past 30 years, the reelection success rate in the House of Representatives was above 95 percent, even with the Republican Revolution in 1994. In the Senate the rate is still above 90 percent. If a member does good work in Congress, eventually he or she gains enough seniority to become a chairman, and then the member can bring home even more "pork" to his or her own constituencies.

It is true that when the general public is polled, people always say they like a balanced budget, but only if it is done on the backs of others. A person with a nice job in the Norfolk shipyards will oppose cutting defense. Those people who sell road-graders say the

country needs more highways. It seems that everyone's grand-
mother is already pauperized and counts on Medicaid to pay for her
nursing home. Similar cases are cited to fight any cuts in Social
Security or Medicare. Clean air and education, according to many
people, is the first interest of government. Basically, the public says
it is willing to cut three items, as people at my town meetings always
told me: welfare, foreign aid, and my own salary as a congressman—
in inverse order, of course! In that respect people are telling us in
polls that even though they may not believe in a free lunch
anymore, they would still like for Congress to balance the budget by
making someone else sacrifice; everyone wants their goodies to
keep coming.

Consequently, members of Congress who spend heavily are
almost always reelected. "Frenzel's First Law" is simply this: The
American people do not name schools after, nor do they raise
statues to, nor do they tear the cuff links off of legislators who say
"no." In other words, they neither criticize nor condemn fiscally
irresponsible legislators. The most popular congressmen are those
who have sponsored programs, who lift people up, and who say that
the United States needs more schools, more space programs, more
defense, more whatever. Meanwhile, those people who advise
caution in spending have been pariahs in the American political
system, at least until the last couple of years. The only reason that
Congress continues to respond to those incentives is because they
work. The system has reelected them, and therefore the system
endures and reelection is almost inevitable.

Whether it always has to be that way is unclear, but in the last
half-dozen years, thinking has begun to change. People are most
concerned that the low savings rate in the United States combined
with the big deficit means that the country has to live off of foreign
capital to build its economy and create jobs for the future. That is
the biggest problem about a deficit. The public will often ask why
Congress is unable to balance the national budget the way individual
citizens have to balance theirs. This attitude is pure balderdash
because private debt has increased much more rapidly than the
federal debt, but at least such rhetoric serves to keep the pressure
on Congress.

Being a representative body, Congress tries to do what the people want it to do. In addition to hearing all of the interest groups pleading to save their pet programs, Congress is now beginning to hear a louder voice from the general taxpayers, saying, "balance that budget or we're going to throw you out!" In the last half-dozen years, the distrust in Congress has risen, as manifested in the change of party control of Congress in 1994. It was not so much that the public loved the Republicans, but that they believed whoever was running the government was not doing a good job. The movement to enact term limits in the United States reflects this general dissatisfaction and desire to get the government off the backs of the people.

All of these factors are tied to the public's nagging worry about the deficit. In plainer terms, the public decided long ago that Congress was sneaky and crooked, but that was tolerable. Now people are worried that Congress is simply incompetent. They cannot understand why Congress cannot balance the budget considering the enormous amount of tax money the government collects. Being labeled as incompetent would be a worse problem for Congress than being corrupt.

The demands for budget-balancing are thus becoming loud enough for Congress to hear. Congressmen are going home and vainly trying to explain to voters all of the reasons why it is so hard to balance the budget, which is only making the situation worse. People are saying that if Congress really wants to balance the budget, it should be able to find a way to do so. Thus far, the problem is that the general public still has a weaker voice than that of the combined interest groups. As I say, though, the times are changing.

Although for years political scientists have predicted that the public was going to "throw the rascals out," perhaps 1994 was the beginning of a real revolution. The change of control of Congress had many causes, but since the new Congress has been in power, reducing deficits has been at least the primary battlefield. The balanced budget amendment was a prime article in the Contract with America, as was the line-item veto. The congressional budget resolution attempts to balance the budget by the year 2002, which this Congress decided was the soonest that it could feasibly deal with the problem. The most important development of all is that President Clinton went against his political advisers and agreed that the budget had to be balanced, but in ten years rather than seven. His position helps to open the window of opportunity a bit wider.

The 1995 budget deficit, at around $160 billion, is going to be the lowest it has been in years. The reasons for the reductions, however, do not necessarily have anything to do with spending policies. Three items are mostly responsible for pulling the deficit below the $200 billion level. First, the economy is strong, and tax receipts have been higher than was anticipated. Second, the federal government is not paying much to bail out the savings and loans associations anymore, so at least for the moment, the government is relieved of that very large expenditure. Third, the first Clinton administration budget included tax increases. Despite this year's drop, the Congressional Budget Office expects deficits to go up again to well over $200 billion each year for the next ten years, during which time the United States will add another $3 trillion or more to the debt. Thus, while there is still some hope, this year's numbers do not indicate that the basic problem has been solved. If Congress follows past spending patterns—and considering the way the budget system is set up, it would be hard to do otherwise—this nation will continue to incur large deficits.

Since we would all like to be optimistic, let's look again at the window of opportunity. The first reason for hope is that the public is becoming angry about deficits and communicating that anger to its representatives. The second reason is that Congress is now in the hands of a political party that is determined to balance the budget. Who knows, however, if the public will stay mad or if the Republicans, particularly those in the Senate, will continue to want to balance the budget?

The third reason for hope is that President Clinton himself has changed his position. To maintain his position, however, he will have to continue to ignore his political advisers, who are giving him the same old story about spend and elect. They are telling the President that he must worry about taking care of the constituencies that elected him, and he is saying that the government must balance the budget. If the Congress and the President continue on their present course, there is a real possibility that deficits will be reduced, if not eliminated.

So far, the Congress has accomplished two of its many necessary tasks. First, it passed a budget resolution that aims to balance the budget by the year 2002, but even though it was passed, do not get your hopes too high on actually getting a balanced budget in seven or even ten years. Those budget projections are done by the Congressional Budget Office (CBO) and the Office of Management and Budget (OMB), respectively, and both offices rely on a good economy over the long term. Both of these budget plans could be wounded by a recession, if not derailed. The main point is to get Congress moving in the proper direction. In addition to having passed the seven-year budget resolution in the House, most of the fiscal 1996 appropriation bills are at least out of committee, and many of them have passed.

By far the most important thing that Congress must accomplish, however, is to pass the reconciliation bill, which allows changes in entitlement programs that cannot be reached through normal appropriations. The problem is whether the House and the Senate can reach an agreement. Both houses want to balance the budget in seven years, but they want to do it in different ways. Therefore, whether or not they can agree on a plan remains in doubt. For example, the Republicans in the Senate backed down and are no longer supporting the House welfare reform proposals, so some savings will be lost there. The House may try to make up those savings with some tax changes that have been labeled corporate welfare by the Democrats and are referred to more delicately by the Republicans as "adjustments" in the tax system.

In the midst of this debate between the House and Senate and between the Congress and the President, the interest groups are marching into battle. They are well-armed, well-trained, and are going to do everything possible to protect their people. Often the advocates are way ahead of the people they are supposed to represent, saying that they cannot possibly accept any cuts. This situation is particularly true with respect to the two largest entitlements for elderly people, Social Security and Medicare. The interest groups seem to be saying that the transfer of wealth from young poor people to old rich people must be continued because God said so on Mount Sinai.

One possible outcome to this budget showdown is the "train wreck" scenario. Actually, two train wrecks are looming. The first one may occur at the end of the fiscal year, 30 September 1995, when all of the appropriations bills are supposed to be on the President's desk. The President has threatened to veto at least eight of the 13 major appropriation bills. To preserve the image of his virility, he will probably have to veto at least a couple of bills. In that case, whatever government agencies that receive funding from those particular appropriations bills will be shut down until a compromise is reached. For instance, if President Clinton vetoes the State Department appropriation, which he claims is inadequate to carry out America's leadership role in the world, then the State Department will be closed, and the employees will not get paid, so they may as well not report to work. That standoff would only be a minor train wreck, though, since no one outside the Beltway would be affected. When civil servants lose a day's pay, usually some kind of compromise is reached quickly. The Treasury Department and the welfare agencies could also be shut down briefly. The train wrecks never close Social Security offices, however. In the Reagan-Bush years, the administration had seven or eight "train wrecks," and as far as I know, there were no casualties and very little dented metal.

The possibility for a more spectacular wreck will come along in mid-October when the Congress must act upon the Congressional Reconciliation Bill, which makes changes in entitlements. The government's ability to borrow money is controlled by federal law. The debt ceiling, which currently stands at 44.9 trillion, will be reached about mid-October. Unless the debt ceiling is extended in the bill, the government cannot borrow any more money and will thus have to close down. Congress intends to give the President the reconciliation bill and the debt ceiling extension in a single package, which is a difficult parliamentary chore.

If the President were to veto that package, there would be a rather severe wreck. Under the precedent established during the Carter administration, the essential business of government could be continued, particularly national security operations and those functions that affected the health and safety of the public. Meat would still be inspected, for example. If the United States were engaged in any wars, they would still be fought. The FBI would stay in business. Much of the rest of the government would close, however, and then people would suffer the consequences.

Why do Americans think that even though there is the possibility of a train wreck, Congress and the President are going to do the right thing? One precedent that provides some hope for us jaded pessimists is that in early 1995, Congress and the President managed to reach a compromise on a bill that called for some rescissions and some supplemental appropriations. The President vetoed the first version because it eliminated certain programs he liked and added ones he disliked. White House officials then sat down and negotiated with Congress until the two sides each agreed to give up a couple of their pet programs. They thus changed the internal mix of programs, but the whole bill came out with the same net savings, which I recall was $16.3 billion.

That scenario is the hope of budgeteers for averting the 30 September and mid-October 1995 train wrecks. The President and Congress will have done some pre-negotiating and will be able to promptly negotiate a compromise that may not satisfy either side but might come close to achieving a balanced budget by the year 2002. I would prefer to balance the budget by 1996, but I will not look a gift horse in the mouth. Anyone who tries to be an odds-maker on the outcome is kidding him- or herself, but some observers of Congress and I estimated that there was about a one-in-three chance that the Congress and the President could agree in 1995 on a plan to balance the budget by 2002; the odds of having a balanced budget are much higher for the year 2005. Thus, some progress will be made in 1995; in fact, some progress has already been made.

It is hard to forecast the future, but whenever the spending growth curves are bent down, further reductions are automatically easier to carry out. The curves no longer point up toward infinity as the old ones did. As an extreme budget hawk who really wants to get rid of the deficits, I see some hope for the first time since I went to Congress. I was elected to Congress in 1970, one year after the last black-ink budget was approved. I have not seen a balanced budget since then, but I think there may be one before I die.

QUESTION: You elucidated this issue very clearly, but you did not mention whether passing a balanced-budget amendment to the Constitution would be truly beneficial or whether it would just postpone tough choices until later.

MR. FRENZEL: I have always thought that a balanced-budget amendment to the Constitution was probably not a great idea. The best such proposal I have ever seen has more words than the entire U.S. Constitution and its amendments. The thought of having seven men and two women in black robes decide on the fiscal policy of the United States worries me, and I think difficulties would arise if the burden of making budget decisions were left to the judicial branch.

Over the years, however, I came to the reluctant conclusion that there is no other way, that only the moral force of the Constitution could make Congress act responsibly. Once Congress passed such a measure by a two-thirds majority and once three-quarters of the states ratified it, only then could Congress impose the necessary sacrifices on its constituents. If the faint hope I raised here today is a valid one, these sacrifices will not be needed, and I will breathe a great sigh of relief. If the budget process does not work out as I suggested, however, I would be forced to push strongly for a balanced-budget amendment. Congress was able to repeal an amendment once in the past, so if there were no other way, it may be necessary to pass a balanced-budget amendment that could be repealed later once men and women of greater fiscal responsibility were elected.

QUESTION: On a panel on which I participated recently, Bill Kristol suggested that if there were a train wreck or an impasse, then the Chief Executive would have to prioritize what is paid and what is not. The revenues would not stop, but the government could not spend more than it receives. Would that plan work?

MR. FRENZEL: It is true that the money keeps coming in, but if it has not been appropriated for a specific purpose, the funds cannot be spent. The President, for example, has vetoed the education, health, and labor bill because there is not enough money to run the programs he favors. If the Congress does not promptly repass the bill, then even if there is money in the treasury and the government still has borrowing authority or incoming tax revenues, the President cannot spend that money. In terms of the reconciliation bill, if the debt ceiling resolution holds up the agreement and the government reaches its budgetary limit but receives tax revenues the next day, there would at least be some money, and the President would have to prioritize the allocation of those funds.

In general, both sides do not worry about handling such emergencies; they usually just snipe at each other. The Congress says that the President is a flint-hearted rascal who vetoed that bill, thus forcing the government to close down. The President counters by saying that Congress is at fault because it did not attempt to set up some procedure that would allow the government to carry on. I look on these train wrecks as political "war dances" that allow each side to articulate the wisdom and virtue of its position. As I suggested earlier, I do not think that "train wrecks" are terribly disruptive. If they enable each side to prove their points and move toward a workable conclusion, they are worthwhile.

QUESTION: Why is the defense budget off the table? Some people suggest that the U.S. government could cut $80 billion from the budget for 1996, and it would not affect the national security at all.

MR. FRENZEL: The United States has been reducing defense expenditures in inflation-adjusted terms every year since fiscal 1987; that is, nine consecutive years of what the economists call "real" reductions. President Clinton, at the urging of the previous Democratic Congress, decided to continue those reductions this year in his budget. They are very modest reductions. When the new Republican Congress came into office, they said the Democrats did not know anything about national security. As a matter of policy included in the Contract with America, the Republicans decided to raise defense expenditures. They are thus at odds with the President. My guess is that once the appropriations process is over, the military budget will be approximately where it was last year, which does not tell people anything about whether the nation is safe or not. The important thing is to decide where the money is being spent, what kinds of plans are being made for the future, and how much training is needed by U.S. troops. Those are the issues that make a difference.

Republicans have always looked at the military budget as "their baby." The way to prove that one was a virile Republican has always been to vote for large defense budgets. Democrats, on the other hand, have always looked at welfare and social programs as a measure of their compassion. The compulsion to spend makes no sense in either party, however.

QUESTION: You spoke about the constituent pressures to raise spending and a little less about the constituent pressures to keep taxes down. Nowadays there is more talk than usual about major reforms of the national tax system. Do you think that such talk holds any promise for addressing the deficit problem?

MR. FRENZEL: I do not. I think it holds great promise for reform of the U.S. tax system, but again, I see a very narrow window of opportunity. Several tax measures have been proposed, such as the Dick Armey flat tax; the Richard Gephardt "un-flat" tax; the Nunn-Domenici consumed income tax; the Lugar sales tax; and Bill Archer, chairman of the Ways and Means Committee, has proposed another version of the sales tax. All of those proposals are different, but they share the purpose of simplifying the system, which many people believe is too complicated.

Tax reform will probably be debated ad nauseam in the next presidential campaign. I would suspect that both candidates, whomever they will be, will almost certainly have a tax reform plank. After the election, whether there is a Republican or Democrat in the White House and no matter which party controls Congress, an attempt will be made to reform the tax system. Of all of the tax proposals that have been presented, none seeks to raise more money than is collected by the current system. They all seem to be based on tax policy rather than fiscal or budgetary policy, so I do not think they help the fiscal deficit problem, at least not as they are being debated at the moment.

QUESTION: Among the people who are ringing the alarm about the budget deficit, who is the most effective? They range from Ross Perot to Warren Rudman and Paul Tsongas's Concord Coalition. Has there been any coalescing of these people behind one forum?

MR. FRENZEL: A coalition has been formed. Whether one is talking about Citizens for a Sound Economy, Citizens Against Government Waste, the National Taxpayers Association, United We Stand America, the Concord Coalition, or the many others, none is more important than the next. They are all crucial in sounding the clarion call that deficits are going to eventually ruin this country. A coalition of a number of these groups has now come together, funded by the Business Roundtable. The intellectual leadership comes from an organization called the Committee for a Responsible Federal Budget. The coalition is not based on any specific deficit reduction plan, but rather they are demanding that the Congress and the President come to some agreement. This group reflects the magical times in which we live when an individual in the United States can really make a difference. Jack Danforth has appeared in television advertisements on behalf of that coalition, and there will be others as well. So far it is not possible to tell whether these groups are doing better in coalition than they were doing individually, but it is worth an attempt.

QUESTION: Robert Reischauer, the former head of CBO, recently argued that as the second "super train wreck" approaches, the President will have the upper hand because of the reconciliation package must-past legislation, with the exception of the debt-limit resolution that you mentioned. Do you think it more likely that the congressional Republicans will blink if the super train wreck in mid-October and the later train wreck occur?

MR. FRENZEL: I think Reischauer is wrong. He is a wonderful man and I have known him for 25 years. He is a great economist, and in fact, I once helped hire him for the post of CBO director. I do not think, however, that anyone has the upper hand in a negotiating situation unless someone believes he or she has the upper hand. It is a matter of whistling by the graveyard, telling yourself how strong you are and how weak the other fellow is. The biggest obstacle to overcome in this negotiation will be getting the House and Senate to come to an agreement on a reconciliation bill. Once they do so, I think they will be stronger than the President.

QUESTION: Do you think the Democratic party may be in danger of suffering a permanent eclipse in the next few years?

MR. FRENZEL: No, but the question is an important one because the Democratic party has gone into a deep, dark funk, and it will take some time for them to get out of it. Whatever is left of the party functionaries is now in Congress. They have rookie leadership in the Senate, but at least that leadership seems to understand the nature of its job and is beginning to look like a real political party. By contrast, in the House there is no indication that the Democratic party understands what a minority party role is or how it should work to get back into the majority. The Democrats who are switching to the Republican side all complain that they would have been perfectly happy to remain Democrats, but they were drummed out of the corps because they were not liberal enough. As Republicans, they at least find that people will listen to them.

Leaders such as Dick Gephardt and Don Bonior, who represent the left-hand edge of the Democratic party, apparently are dreaming that they are going to come out of retirement like Pancho Villa and conquer Mexico, but they aren't! They have to start building a new party. The Rooseveltian coalition, if it is not already dead, is in the casket with a big stake in its heart, and they do not seem to know how to get it out. The first sign of life will be when the Democrats in Congress begin to learn how to work with their President. You are listening to the voice of experience; I had to cast many votes for Richard Nixon when it was unpleasant to do so. A party has no strength unless its members stick together. As far as the Democratic caucus in Congress is concerned, Clinton has the measles on many issues. Someday they are going to have to stand up and cast some tough votes in support of their president or they are always going to be weak and feeble. I expect another half-dozen years of difficulty for the Democrats because I think they need new leaders, and I do not think they will get them very soon. Certainly Bill Clinton will be renominated by his party. There is talk of Dick Gephardt not being reelected as leader of the House Democrats, but there are no candidates running against him. These situations have to change. Democrats are in difficulty and need help.

I don't think a new party will be formed. Historically, third parties in America have a colorful tradition, but not a successful one. The last major new party in the United States emerged in the 1850s, and that was the Republican party. I think both parties are currently rather weak, but the Democrats are really in trouble.

QUESTION: Would a line-item veto in fact be conducive to a higher degree of fiscal responsibility? Couldn't the President use it as a political club to gain support? For example, he might say something like, "If you don't vote for my health plan you won't get a new post office in your district."

MR. FRENZEL: Tom Foley has always raised that thesis. He said it is not a fiscal tool, but a *political* tool, using the example that the President might cut Washington state's wheat subsidies out of the budget unless Foley cooperated in appropriating more military money. That outcome is possible, and it does not bother me. I have served in legislatures practically all of my life, both in state and national government, and I have always felt it was an unequal battle. The chief executive was always overmatched, so I do not mind giving him a little more power. The line-item veto would certainly be both a fiscal and a political tool, but I think it is worth taking the political risk to put a little more fiscal power in the hands of the president. Congress, however, is unlikely to give the current president the line-item veto, so perhaps we are just speaking academically.

QUESTION: Are the Republicans in Congress likely to subject themselves to danger by appearing to validate the currently popular slogan, "Take welfare money from the poor and give it to the rich in the form of a tax cut"?

MR. FRENZEL: I think that is a possible outcome. There is a general political rule that when down on one's luck, as the Democrats are now, don't worry because the other party will soon screw up and your party will be back on top. I remember the Watergate days vividly, and suddenly my crowd is now back on top. The worm turns quickly.

I have to acknowledge that the United States has had a "plateau" development, with perhaps as many as three-quarters of the population enjoying only about the same level of real income as they had 20 years ago. Meanwhile, on top of the scale, the income levels have risen much more sharply. That situation is dangerous in any society anywhere. On the other hand, raising the issue is a two-edged sword for the Democrats because for the last three years, they have had no ideological weapon except class warfare, which is not a big seller. People may agree with it, but only "crunch issues" influence the vote either way. In fact, Democrats are likely to sound rather whiny on the subject. They need issues with a great deal more moral force than class warfare to make their point.

With respect to taxation, one can make the point that the government would indeed be giving money to rather wealthy people under this tax-cut proposal, and it would be taking from poor people in terms of welfare cuts. The obvious solution to that problem is for Congress to compromise with the President on the income level for the tax cut. My guess is that they will be eager to do so because even though they realize that the class warfare argument is not a strong one, it does make them wince. My guess is they will reduce the income level to about $100,000 and maybe even less for those eligible to take the child-care tax reduction. That way, even if there is a capital gains cut, people in the various income brackets will still be paying approximately the same percentage of taxes as they did before the tax cut.

QUESTION: You said that the goal of achieving a balanced budget by the years 2002 or 2005 could be upset by a recession between now and then. Is that because the government would receive less revenues during a recession, or is it because the government would try to stimulate the economy by spending more money?

MR. FRENZEL: Both.

QUESTION: Is there a particular time that the economy should be stimulated? Is a stimulus program appropriate in times of stagflation? Should the government stimulate the economy during a recession, or should it wait until the recession becomes a depression? Is there a particular percentage of economic contraction that should trigger increased government spending?

MR. FRENZEL: The question of when and by how much the economy should be stimulated depends on whether one is a Keynesian, a monetarist, or a supply-sider, or anything else. All budget projections are based on economic assumptions, and now the CBO's economic assumptions call for a steady growth rate of a little more than 2 percent over that seven-year period. One of the problems with the President's ten-year plan is that the OMB projections predict a somewhat higher rate of growth. So the President assumes that more tax revenue will be brought in and less will be spent on the safety net programs than Congress has proposed. If both of those assumptions are wrong because the country has a couple of down years or flat years, then there will be less tax revenue and more spending, and the budget will not be balanced on schedule. If the spending patterns are modified, however, the government will eventually make up for the shortfall once the economy begins to improve again.

The question of when to stimulate the economy and when not to is much more complicated. Congress has discovered over the past 20 years that the old Keynesian stimulus policy of building more highways or more public works is rather feeble. It results in paying much more overtime wages to the construction trades, but it does not create many new jobs.

With respect to supply-side tax cuts, supply-side theories are valid up to a point, but no one except for supply-siders such as Jack Kemp or Jude Wanniski really knows what that point is. Most economists are happier with a skillfully managed monetary policy;

that is, if the Federal Reserve knows when to cut interest rates and so forth. No one is perfect at monitoring policy. A variety of economic policy combinations are possible. I have my own preferences, but they are wholly subjective.

QUESTION: What, if any, complications are brought about by the presidential campaign during this window of opportunity?

MR. FRENZEL: The answer to that question is not yet known. The Senate is clearly becoming much more competitive, particularly between two of the candidates, Senators Gramm and Dole. In the reshuffling after the Bob Packward departure, Senator Gramm was trying hard to be assigned to the Finance Committee so he would be in a position to push for a larger tax cut. Meanwhile, Senator Dole is looking for someone with more seniority than Senator Gramm to serve on the committee. This competition will have several ramifications, and at the moment it is hard to know what is happening. Some conservatives are worried about Senator Dole being supported by moderate senators, fearing that he will tend to compromise on the budget debates to keep their support and thus lose some precious opportunities. I do not take that point of view. The Senate is already on record as being committed to a 2002 deficit elimination date, so that will not be a problem. Overall, presidential campaigns do louse up national policy-making, however.

QUESTION: How much support does Phil Gramm have, especially in light of his controversy with Senator Dole?

MR. FRENZEL: I am not an expert in presidential campaigns. I think I am the only man in Congress who did not believe he would become president someday, so I have never worried about it a great deal. I cannot rate the candidates' prospects. Dole seems to be the favorite now; it is his race to lose. Senator Gramm seems to be running second among people who will go to Republican state conventions or vote in Republican primaries, but he has never made it into double-digit figures. The candidate in first place tries to keep the ship on a steady course. If a candidate is in second place, he or she must usually pull some stunt to grab publicity. The danger in this situation is that Senator Gramm may get nasty with Senator Dole, which he almost has to do to improve his position. For the moment, I would say that Senator Gramm's position is not very good. Some people in Washington have suggested that even candidates who are further down the list are more likely to be the second-to-last survivor rather than Senator Gramm. With Dole being somewhat right of center and Gramm being far right of center, someone such as Pete Wilson who is perceived as being left of the Republican center would be a more likely alternative.

NARRATOR: We have had a political and intellectual feast, as those of us who have heard our speaker on other occasions knew it would be, and we thank Mr. Frenzel.

« CHAPTER 8 »

THE FEDERAL BUDGET DEFICIT*

ROBERT J. SAMUELSON

NARRATOR: Robert J. Samuelson received his bachelor's degree in government from Harvard University in 1967. From 1967 to 1973 he was a reporter for the *Washington Post*, covering business and economics. In 1976, after four years as a free-lance writer, Mr. Samuelson was appointed economics correspondent for the *National Journal* and began writing a weekly national column for the *Washington Post* and other newspapers. Since 1984 he has written a biweekly column for *Newsweek*, which was recently syndicated by the Washington Post Writers Group. Mr. Samuelson has received the National Magazine Award and three Gerald Loeb awards for distinguished business and economics journalism. His recent book, *The Good Life and Its Discontents: The American Dream in the Age of Entitlement, 1945–1995*, has received national attention for its timely subject. Mr. Samuelson will speak today on the budget deficit and its effect on the U.S. economy.

MR. SAMUELSON: When Ken Thompson invited me to speak here last fall, I wondered what I was going to talk about since I assumed that Congress and the White House would have already

---

Presented in a Forum at the Miller Center of Public Affairs on 6 February 1996.

reached an agreement to balance the budget. The fact that there is still no budget agreement makes the theme of this talk both more relevant and more timely than it would have been otherwise. What I will discuss today is the transformation of the federal budget from a political document—used as a framework for making political decisions—into something mainly seen as a tool of economic policy. This transformation is the central reason why the U.S. government has had budget deficits in every year since 1960, with the one exception of 1969. This constant string of deficits coincides with a change in the way Americans think about the budget. Until the 1960s, balancing the budget was an American political tradition. The budget was regarded as one way by which to define the nature of government, set its priorities, and then pay for its choices with the appropriate taxes levied on the people. Balancing the budget was simply considered a matter of political prudence. As James Savage from the University of Virginia argues in his superb book, *Balanced Budgets and American Politics*:

> The balanced budget idea, embodied in the concept of "corruption," guided public policy not only on budgetary matters but also on such related issues as administrative growth, "internal improvements" [such as roads and harbors], the nature of currency, banking, tariffs, national defense, and especially federal-state relations. Borrowed from classical and English political thought, the concept of corruption became uniquely American. . . . In the American context, balanced budgets originally assumed their symbolic characteristics in the years of Jeffersonian and Jacksonian democracy. A balanced national budget signified a popular willingness and ability to limit the purpose and size of the federal government, to restrain its influence in the economy, to protect states' rights, to maintain the Constitution's balance of powers, and to promote republican virtue.[*]

In short, until the 1960s balancing the budget was a well-established tradition considered to be a matter of common sense.

---

[*]James D. Savage, *Balanced Budgets and American Politics* (Ithaca, N.Y.: Cornell University Press, 1988).

This thinking did not mean that a balanced budget was always achieved. In times of war, the U.S. government hardly ever balanced the budget. During periods of economic decline, the budget likewise usually went into deficit. Even when the budget remained in surplus, the surplus might drop sharply because Congress could not act quickly enough to raise the revenues (through higher taxes and tariffs) needed to offset the effects of the downturn. Thus, the notion that the U.S. government became very sophisticated in the late 20th century and began to calibrate swings in the budget according to the business cycle is ahistorical. Swings in the budget balance also occurred in earlier eras. The overriding point is that even though the United States ran deficits during wars and periods of economic decline, Americans still regarded the budget as a political instrument throughout the 1950s and held the belief that the budget ought to be balanced. It is interesting that this widespread conviction survived the Great Depression and World War II despite the fact that the U.S. government never ran a balanced budget during those periods.

The balanced budget ideal provided a discipline for government in which politicians were forced to weigh the cost of imposing extra taxes against the anticipated benefit of extra public spending. It was a useful discipline in that it forced officials to take the responsibility for making fundamental decisions regarding the proper role and size of government. In other words, before 1960 there was a well-developed political principle guiding budget debates. Most of this discipline was lost, however, beginning in the 1960s. The budget began to be used as a tool for economic policy: to improve the economy's performance, to raise the rate of growth, and perhaps also to alter the distribution of income. In the 1960s, it was often argued that deficits are good for the economy. After 1960, decisions on whether to have a deficit, balance the budget, or even run a surplus had to be justified in economic terms. All of the past tradition was discarded to make room for what was thought to be more enlightened, sophisticated, and modern economic thinking. Once such a long-standing tradition is destroyed, however, it is very difficult to reestablish.

Over the last 30 years or so, there has been a succession of economic theories and arguments about the effects of the budget on the economy, none of which has become firmly established enough to provide an alternative to the previous political framework. Since no convincing economic reason to balance the budget exists, the political vacuum has allowed politicians to do what is politically easiest–to spend more and tax less. For that reason deficits have essentially become a permanent condition of American government.

The first theory that defended deficit spending was Keynesianism. The basic idea is very simple. It says, in essence, that whenever economists detect that the economy is going into a slump, the government should intervene by raising expenditures or cutting taxes to stimulate the economy until full employment is achieved. In either case, the ultimate result is a budget deficit. In short, Keynesians believed that it was possible to eliminate the business cycle–the pain and inconvenience of having to endure recessions–by running a countercyclical fiscal policy through the government's tax and spending.

In practice, however, Keynesianism failed. It may be that the theory is fundamentally flawed, but even if it were not, it proved impossible to put into practice. First, economists were not able–and may never be able–to predict every recession before it happens or identify one early enough to implement the necessary corrective tax and spending policies. Economists' tools have never been equal to the theory. Even if they were, there is still a practical problem of political asymmetry with Keynesianism. Congress and presidents are happy to cut taxes and raise spending, which are always politically popular. Politicians are much less eager to raise taxes and cut spending, however, and that is what the Keynesian theory calls for when the economy is "overheating." Since the goal of Keynesianism was not simply to prevent recessions but to navigate the economy along a path of constant growth without high or rising inflation, there was a natural and unavoidable asymmetry built into this system. The practical consequence of trying to avoid recessions through increased spending and lower taxes was an increase in the annual rate of inflation from 1 to 2 percent in 1960 to a peak of almost 14 percent in 1980 and 1981. These policies may have had the effect of postponing recessions, but they certainly did not avoid them. The recessions of 1973-1975 and 1981-1982 were the most severe in the postwar era, and their severity was directly related to the preexisting inflation, which was in turn caused by the government's expansionary monetary and fiscal policies. It is often argued that in an ideal world, the federal government, like many state governments, would have a capital budget; that is, a separate set of accounts for long-term investments. In the absence of such a formal capital account, our current practice of running continual deficits supposedly acts as a kind of crude substitution.

A second idea that is used to justify deficit spending is that the government, like private industry, needs to borrow money to make capital investments that are expected to yield social and economical benefits. As long as the projected rate of return on these investments is higher than the cost of capital, then the U.S. government is justified in borrowing money to invest in research and development, infrastructure, education, health care, and so forth. But what exactly is an "investment"? In practice it is hard to define. For example, Robert Eisner, an economist at Northwestern and past president of the American Economics Association, argues that government spending on health care should be considered as an investment for the future. There is no doubt that this type of spending is appropriate in some cases. For instance, money spent by the government to help improve the health of a four-year-old child from a low-income family is an investment. Most government spending on health care, however, is spent on older Americans and their long-term care in nursing homes through Medicare or Medicaid. That kind of spending is not an investment in the future; it is consumption.

There is also an ongoing debate among economists as to how much money spent on education is an investment for the future and how much of it is consumption. I would consider a large part of a college education as consumption because it is not solely related to future earning power; it also prepares students to appreciate life in the broadest sense. There are questions about how the government's research and development expenditures should be accounted for as well. Some people in the business world think that R&D ought to be immediately expensed and not amortized over time. Obviously, these are all difficult technical issues. Even if there were a capital budget, however, politicians would still want to spend more and tax less and would therefore put everything they could into the "investment" account. The capital budget would just give them an excuse to do what is politically convenient. As with the Keynesian theory, the investment argument is appealing when considered in the abstract. As a practical matter, though, it is utterly bankrupt, and if it were adopted by the federal government, it would raise the gimmickry of "smoke and mirrors" budgeting to a new and unprecedented level.

A third argument used to justify deficits is supply-side economics. First used in the 1980s, this theory is making a comeback in the debate over the flat tax proposal. Supply-side economics is a predominately conservative theory, based on the idea that if tax rates are cut sufficiently, then the free market economy becomes unburdened from the oppressive hand of government, thereby leading to an explosion of economic growth. As a result of the increase in GNP, some or all of the tax revenues that were lost by cutting the tax rates would be made up by the larger tax base. As with the Keynesian and capital-budget arguments, this argument is appealing but has little real substance. When supply-side economic policies were implemented in the 1980s, they failed to produce the expected outcome. Before Reagan came into office, the top marginal income tax rate was 70 percent. In spite of substantial tax cuts culminating in the 1986 Tax Reform Act (which lowered the highest rate to 28 percent), the rate of economic growth only improved slightly during the Reagan years. It is more likely that the improvement in growth in the 1980s is attributable to other factors, such as lower inflation, an increase in competition in the economy, and an improvement in corporate management. Although the tax cuts may have had a beneficial effect, there was not enough economic growth to cover the loss of all or even most of the revenues that resulted from lowering taxes in the first place. The extravagant notion that supply-side tax cuts could pay for themselves has been disproved by the persistent deficits of the 1980s.

Thus, none of the three common arguments as to why deficits are good for us holds up under dispassionate scrutiny. One might ask, if all of the asserted economic reasons for running deficits are so flimsy, why don't we just go ahead and balance the budget? Ironically, the answer is exactly the same: The economic reasons for balancing the budget are not very strong either. Without a convincing argument, it is very difficult to raise taxes or cut spending.

The most common argument made in favor of balancing the budget is that it would dramatically lower interest rates: people's mortgage payments, car payments, and payments on student loans would drop significantly. This effect is considered by politicians to be a concrete, tangible benefit for doing something that would otherwise be politically unpopular. Although it is true that lower deficits or budget surpluses would have a tendency to reduce interest rates (and higher deficits tend to increase them), there are many factors that influence interest rates besides budget deficits. The most important factor in determining long-term interest rates is inflation and inflationary expectations. For example, inflation rose sharply in the 1970s and people began to fear that this was a permanent phenomenon. As a result, long-term interest rates increased substantially because lenders and investors wanted to be compensated for the erosion of the value of their money. As inflation came down in the 1980s and as people became convinced that this decline was permanent, interest rates fell. Because there was somewhat of a lag between changes in the current rate of inflation and expectations of future inflation, interest rates have declined rather slowly in reaction to the lower inflation. Nevertheless, inflation is *the* main influence on interest rates, in my view. Consider a hypothetical example.

Suppose that tomorrow morning the budget were somehow balanced and at the same time, inflation increased from its current rate of 2 to 3 percent up to 10 percent. Would anyone doubt that the interest rates would also increase substantially? Again, I am not arguing that deficits have no effect on interest rates. Rather, I am saying that the effect is not obvious and is not easily measurable. It is certainly not something that honestly can be portrayed as a benefit from reducing the deficits.

A second argument often made for lowering the budget deficit is that doing so will raise our future incomes and living standards. The basic concept behind this theory is that government borrowing crowds out private borrowing and therefore reduces private investment, which is a major engine of economic growth, greater efficiencies, and ultimately, higher living standards. A lower investment base, presumably, will result in a lower standard of living.

Over the long term, there is something to this argument. Up until now, though, there has not been much evidence in support of it. First, over the past four decades private business investment, not including housing, has risen consistently in relation to the overall economy. In the 1950s Americans invested 9.7 percent of the gross domestic product (GDP); in the 1960s, 10 percent; in the 1970s, 11.2 percent; and in the 1980s, 12.1 percent. As these figures show, private business investment is not actually declining. The explanation for this increase in investment is that the United States ran a trade deficit in the 1970s and 1980s and in effect has been able as a society to invest more and to consume more at the same time. In short, the theoretical argument that large deficits would crowd out investment has not come to pass, in large part because the dollar is the world's reserve currency. In effect, the United States sends dollars abroad, and other countries ship their goods back to the United States. Although the deficits have crowded out national savings to a certain extent, they have not yet crowded out national investment.

Even if government borrowing did crowd out some investment, it is not clear that it would have a significant effect on living standards. The United States has a business capital base—including machines, equipment, buildings, computers, airlines, and so on—of about $12 trillion. Every year, that amount increases by approximately $800 billion in new investment. If it were raised by 1 percentage point of GDP, only $70 billion would be added. Thus, even if the annual rate of investment were increased substantially, it would not add a significant amount to the U.S. capital base. The productivity of society and of the economy depends on how efficiently Americans invest and how well they use the existing capital base, not simply the rate of investment. Two practical examples illustrate my point. First, in the 1980s the United States wasted a great deal of capital by investing in new construction of office buildings, shopping centers, and hotels that no one needed. Second, even though the former Soviet Union used to have a rate of investment twice the American rate, they did not reap much benefit from it. The Soviets poured out agricultural machinery that then sat abandoned in fields, while many of their factories did not produce anything at all. Although the crowding out argument is theoretically attractive and has some validity, what is most important for raising living standards in the long run is how efficiently Americans invest their savings and how well they use their accumulated capital base. Increasing business investment might ultimately raise economic growth 0.1 to 0.3 percent a year. Such an increase, although quite significant over the long term, is not something politicians can sell to win an election.

A third reason given in support of balancing the budget is that running constant deficits tends to be inflationary. This argument is plausible, based on the experiences of many countries that financed their large budget deficits by having their central bank print more money. Consequently, it is quite conceivable that large deficits would lead to rising inflation, but it is not inevitable, at least not under American conditions. In fact, over the past ten years the United States has experienced rising deficits with falling inflation, so that argument has proved to be invalid with regard to the United States. Thus, all the alleged benefits and catastrophes that people predicted would result from running deficits have failed to come true. Without a valid economic argument for balancing the budget, politicians have continued to do what is easiest: spend more than they tax. It really is that simple.

Nevertheless, I do believe that the U.S. government ought to balance the budget and go back to the tradition of fiscal prudence that prevailed before 1960. The folk wisdom that governed the budget for almost two centuries should be revived in order to build a framework that forces our legislators to make political choices about the nature of government, the size of government, and the proper role of government in American society. Washington needs the discipline of a framework by which to calibrate pain versus gain within the context of a political climate in which many Americans are suspicious of government but still want many of the benefits that government provides.

Without a return to fiscal prudence, the United States will sooner or later face serious economic consequences. Running large deficits indefinitely raises the risk that the United States may experience some sort of economic crisis. Europe, by the way, is already showing symptoms of this condition. At some point, foreign financial markets will begin to charge a premium in interest rates because they will not believe that the U.S. debt is worth its face value. As interest rates rise, it will become harder and harder for the United States to service the debt. Creditors will come to fear that the U.S. government will either inflate its way out of debt or will default.

Even if there were no economic consequences of continuing deficits, Americans would still need to make political choices about the role of government in the future. The current situation is politically unsustainable. Over the postwar period, the federal budget has evolved essentially from an instrument of national security policy into an instrument of social welfare policy. In the mid-1950s, defense spending accounted for two-thirds of the federal budget. Today it is about 17 percent, and by the early part of the next century, it is projected to be between 13 and 15 percent. Defense spending is clearly becoming a less important part of the budget.

Meanwhile, social spending has increased, primarily consisting of benefits for older Americans through Medicare and Social Security. When these programs were enacted, there were more workers per retiree than there are today and life expectancy was lower. Early in the next century baby boomers will reach the age of retirement. If these programs are left in place without modification, tax rates will have to go through the ceiling to provide sufficient funding. I am talking about an increase in the tax burden of somewhere between 30 and 50 percent. In current dollar terms, that is an increase of approximately $400–$800 billion annually. People will not tolerate such an increase.

There are only two alternatives to a massive tax hike. One is to let the deficit rise to at least twice as large a proportion of GDP as it has been in recent years. The second option is to dramatically cut Social Security and Medicare benefits, which strikes me as unfair to those who are just about to retire. It would be much better to begin setting new rules now and gradually implement them over a period of 15 years. If the minimum retirement age is to be further raised, people deserve a fair warning. All of these choices would be extraordinarily disruptive, both socially and politically.

The only way to avoid such an anguishing predicament is to reclaim the old folk wisdom and balance the budget.

QUESTION: How will Congress balance the budget?

MR. SAMUELSON: It will not be that difficult in my opinion. There are some programs we simply do not need anymore. For example, does anyone think that people in the United States would starve if we did not have farm subsidies? Why are farmers more deserving of income support than magazine columnists or anyone else? I also do not think the National Endowment for the Arts is needed, although many people would disagree.

Another way to balance the budget is to give some programs back to the states. There is no justification for having the federal government subsidize local mass transit, for instance. If Los Angeles wants to build a mass transit system, then that city's residents should pay for it, not the people in Montana, New York, or Maryland.

Yet even if all of the unnecessary programs were eliminated or given to the states, the budget would still not be balanced. The growth of some of the larger programs such as Social Security and Medicare needs to be checked. What the Republicans proposed in their budget for Medicare this year was for the most part a very sensible approach to deficit reduction, and it is a tragedy that the President chose to demagogue this issue. Beginning in the year 2000, the retirement age needed to qualify for Social Security benefits will be raised to 67, but it should be raised to 70 by the time the baby boomers retire. Congress should also implement means tests for Social Security recipients. In 1935, and even as recently as 1965, most people who were over 65 were poor almost by definition; that is not the case anymore. By instituting these regulations in an incremental manner, the government can get the growth of these programs under control, and it will thus be easier to balance the budget.

QUESTION: Would a balanced-budget amendment be practical?

MR. SAMUELSON: I am against a balanced-budget amendment, not for technical reasons, but because I do not believe the U.S. Constitution should be amended on a casual whim. Congress could pass a balanced-budget if its members had the will to do so. If a balanced-budget amendment were passed, Congress would find some way around it, and then not only would the United States have a political problem, it would have a constitutional problem as well. I have likewise been opposed to the school prayer amendment and the equal rights amendment. Such attempts to put legislation into the Constitution invariably entail anticipating the many ways that a proposed amendment could be circumvented. This misguided approach would undermine the legitimacy of the Constitution, which is supposed to be an expression of our country's basic principles.

QUESTION: Would you comment on the flat-tax debate?

MR. SAMUELSON: I am against the idea of a flat tax, as well. It fosters the illusion that if Congress made a dramatic change in the tax system, economic growth would somehow increase so dramatically that all these difficult political choices would be washed away by the flood of new tax revenues. *Flat tax* is merely a code word for tax cut, just as the term *supply-side economics* was. Nevertheless, I believe that much of the deep frustration people feel toward the complexity and perversity of the U.S. tax system is justified. Congress could bring the top rates back down to close to where they were after the 1986 Tax Reform Act. The flat tax, however, is a deceptive distraction from the main problem. Reprioritizing government spending programs and balancing the budget would have a much greater effect on reducing the future tax burden.

QUESTION: In a democracy, how can special interest groups such as the farmers be prevented from using their political power to stop the elimination of the dozens of government spending programs that are not in the broad public interest?

MR. SAMUELSON: A number of political approaches have been suggested to deal with this dilemma, but none of them have been very effective. The argument most often made is that budget reform cannot be done gradually. Farmers might be willing in an abstract sense to give up their subsidies if they thought it would contribute to realizing the larger goal of balancing the budget, but they are not willing to give them up simply as a matter of casual sacrifice. In other words, if such programs are eliminated in isolation on a piecemeal basis, the money might simply be redirected to some other undeserving group. Farmers could complain that they are just as deserving as anyone else. The only way to achieve reform with government subsidy programs is for them to be made as one package. Justice demands that the burden of sacrifice be shared. The American people desperately need political leaders with both the practical skill and the heartfelt desire to accomplish this goal.

NARRATOR: We have been privileged to hear Mr. Samuelson speak on the U.S. deficit problem and are grateful for the opportunity. Many thanks.

IV

THE POLITICAL STRUGGLE FOR
THE DEBT AND THE DEFICIT

CHAPTER 9

THE GOP REVOLUTION AND THE BATTLE OVER THE BUDGET[*]

DAVID MARANISS

NARRATOR: David Maraniss, who has been a reporter for the *Washington Post* since 1977, began his writing career as a student at the University of Wisconsin where he wrote for the *Madison Capital Times*. He came by his writing inclination naturally, as his grandfather was a printer, his father a newspaper editor, and his mother a book review editor. Since his writing career began, he has written thousands of articles and won several awards.

Mr. Maraniss covered Maryland politics for the first two years of his career at the *Washington Post*, after which he became Maryland editor, deputy Metro editor, and Metro editor. He returned to reporting in 1983 and won the Newspaper Guild Front Page Award for "The Committee," plus a year-long series on the House Energy and Commerce Committee. He moved to Austin, Texas, as the *Washington Post*'s Southwest bureau chief and covered national politics as well regional politics. In 1989 he and Rick Atkinson were awarded the Hancock Prize for "The $150 Billion Catastrophe," a series of articles on the savings and loan scandal. In 1990 he won the Gold Medal of the National Conference of

---

Presented in a Forum at the Miller Center of Public Affairs on 3 June 1996.

Christians and Jews for "Hard Choices in Black and White," his series on integration in American institutions. For his articles on Bill Clinton during the 1992 presidential campaign, he won the 1993 Pulitzer Prize for National Reporting.

Mr. Maraniss last spoke at the Miller Center about his biography of Bill Clinton entitled, *First in His Class* (1995). In his discussion of the politics of the debt and deficit today, he will draw from his new book, *"Tell Newt to Shut Up!"*, co-authored with fellow *Washington Post* reporter Michael Weisskopf. This book is based upon their prize-winning series of articles on this subject that appeared in the *Post*. For a relatively young national affairs journalist, Maraniss has had a spectacular career. We are honored that he would return to the Miller Center to discuss this highly important subject.

MR. MARANISS: When I spoke at the Miller Center 14 months ago, the world was very different. Bill Clinton was struggling to prove that he was relevant, while Newt Gingrich was on top of the world, endeavoring to govern the country from Capitol Hill; his revolution was streaming forward. The Republicans were in the midst of pushing through the entire Contract With America at that point, and the conventional wisdom was that after only two years in office, Bill Clinton would be a long shot for reelection. Based on my study of the previous cycles of loss and recovery in President Clinton's life, however, I said then that it was much too early to count Clinton out. In the years since then, a remarkable turnabout has indeed taken place.

In the year since I was last at the Miller Center, I have spent almost every day working on Capitol Hill with my closest friend and colleague at the *Washington Post*, Michael Weisskopf. Over the course of the year we wrote 14 articles in a series called "Inside the Revolution," covering all major aspects of policy that the Republicans were trying to change after taking over the House for the first time in 40 years. Our first story revealed that lobbyists for some of the major corporations in America came in on the coattails of the House Republican revolutionaries and immediately began drafting laws to cut back on environmental regulation.

Our series of articles was based on diaries and notes we had taken from meetings with major figures in the House, from Speaker Gingrich down to low-level aides. We made a practice of calling all of the people in the story before it was published and telling them exactly what information and quotes we had gathered from them and how the material would be used. The Republicans did not necessarily like everything we wrote, but they knew we were being utterly fair with them, which allowed us to maintain the contacts we had developed. As the year progressed, we found ourselves truly on the "inside of the revolution," to the point that when the crunch came in the final months of the balanced-budget fight, Michael and I were receiving daily reports of new developments to which no other reporters had access. From this raw material our book *"Tell Newt to Shut Up!"* evolved.

My biography of President Clinton, *First in His Class*, had described several of the personality elements that helped the President in his startling political comeback. Likewise, those elements precipitating Speaker Gingrich's collapse are covered in this latest book, *"Tell Newt to Shut Up!"*. My two books thus began to converge in explaining what was going on in Washington during that final battle over the federal deficit and the balanced budget.

As a journalist trying to become a biographer and a historian, I find that the motivations behind people's actions and the forces that shape them are what fascinate me the most. Economists could, of course, provide a more sophisticated analysis of the policy issues. It is hard to overemphasize the hubris that Newt Gingrich and his supporters brought to Washington when they took over Congress in January 1995. They really believed that they were going to change the world, and every committee assignment and policy change made reflected the unswerving conviction that their decisions were the right ones. The book we wrote begins by examining Newt Gingrich's sense of how he would take over and his lack of understanding of how his own world had changed:

> Sonny Bono got it first. Before most professional image advisers and veteran Republican pols had a clue, the freshman congressman from Palm Springs anticipated what would happen. Newt Gingrich was rocketing into a new realm, and he seemed to

have no idea how different and dangerous it would be. It mattered little that he had prepared himself to be the Speaker of the U.S. House of Representatives since his college days, or that he had spent thousands of hours with managers at Delta, Coca-Cola, Ford, and the Army studying how large institutions operated. Everything he had learned about leadership from examining the careers of FDR, Churchill, and Reagan was secondary now to one unavoidable fact that a mustachioed little guy who crooned "I Got You Babe" with Cher intuitively understood when others did not.

Bono issued his warning on the morning the world changed: January 4, 1995. Sonny's first day as congressman. Newt's first day as speaker. The revolution was already in full, dizzying swirl. Newt was marching from meeting to interview to speech with the bearing of an overstuffed field general, surrounded by the hubbub scrum of aides, photographers, and press hacks. As he and Bob Dole, majority leader of the Senate, were leaving a CBS Morning News interview in the old Agriculture Committee Room in the Longworth House Office Building, Bono approached them. The singer-cum-pol was scheduled to become the network's next guest, but before he went on the air he had a word of advice for his new boss. What Newt was feeling now, he said, was what Sonny felt the first time he cut a hit record. You dream and dream and dream and then all of a sudden it happens so fast.

"You're a celebrity now," he told Gingrich. "The rules are different for celebrities. I know it. I've been there. I've been a celebrity. I used to be a bigger celebrity. But let me tell you, you're not being handled right. This is not political news coverage. This is celebrity status. You need handlers. You need to understand what you're doing. You need to understand the attitude of the media towards celebrities."

Gingrich barely listened. This was the biggest day of his life. No time for alarms, especially not from Sonny Bono.

"Yeah," he said distractedly. "We'll get around to that."

In fact, Newt Gingrich never did "get around to that," which is the root of our book's title.

To understand what eventually happened to the struggle to achieve a balanced budget, it is important first to understand the extent to which the Republican revolution became identified with one person and one personality. The title of the book is a comment that was made not by any Democrat in Congress, but by Gingrich's best friends in Congress, the House Republicans. Following the trip to Israel for Yitzhak Rabin's funeral in November 1995, Gingrich complained that President Clinton would not talk to him on the airplane and that he had to leave through the back door. The same week, he had connected a brutal murder in Chicago to the failings of the welfare system. These incidents followed a series of verbal gaffes on Gingrich's part over the course of that year. After the Thanksgiving break, John Boehner, the House Republican conference chairman, was delegated the task of speaking to Gingrich about the situation. He told Gingrich that their constituents still believed in the Republicans and thought they were doing the right thing but the same constituents were telling their representatives, "Please tell Newt to shut up!" Gingrich did temporarily "bench" himself, but he could not keep his mouth closed for long.

The Republicans were not only relying too heavily on one person—Newt Gingrich—to lead them; they were also relying on one political strategy: the balanced budget. In February 1995, when the Republicans realized how the difficult it would be to get a balanced-budget amendment through the Senate, Speaker Gingrich announced that the House would pass a bill to balance the budget in seven years, thus making such an amendment to the Constitution unnecessary. He was following advice given by people outside of Congress. Corporate chiefs whom he invited to dinners in the Speaker's office were telling him that in order to downsize an organization, one had to boldly plunge ahead and just do it. In embracing this advice, he told House Budget Committee Chairman John Kasich that the budget would be balanced in seven years no matter what.

This position took Kasich by surprise. As a Republican from Ohio with a keen sense of humor and a true commitment to balancing the budget, Kasich had not anticipated that in his first year as the budget chairman he would actually have to pull off a resolution to balance the budget in seven years. He warned Gingrich that reaching that goal would require unprecedented changes in the Medicare system. Nonetheless, over the course of that spring and early summer, the Republicans managed to push through their seven-year balanced-budget plan.

Meanwhile, certain problems were emerging within the Republican side of the House. As the majority party for the first time in 40 years, they faced the "big tent" problems that the Democrats had been facing since the New Deal: They had to reconcile the agendas of different factions, something which they were not accustomed to doing as a minority. To gain support for their seven-year balanced-budget plan, the moderate and conservative wings of the party had to be dealt with in turn to mediate disputes on issues ranging from abortion funding to federal regulations of the workplace and the environment. These disputes came to a head in early August during the struggle to pass the controversial Labor–Health and Human Services (HHS) appropriations bill.

Newt Gingrich was actually a moderating force during most of that struggle. Many people think of him as a conservative firebrand, but when he came into power as the Speaker of the House, his personality had to change if he was to govern and deal with factions within his own party. Many of the freshmen as well as Majority Leader Richard Armey and Majority Whip Tom DeLay were far more conservative than Gingrich. The passage of the Labor–HHS bill, the largest of the appropriations bills, was considered a massive victory for Gingrich and his troops because they had successfully held all of the Republican factions together and pushed through this bill that made a historic change in the way government dealt with social services.

The night they passed this bill, Gingrich and his top friends celebrated until 3:00 a.m. in Dick Armey's office. Speaker Gingrich compared the victory to the British army's maneuvering against the French during the Peninsular War, which set the stage for the Duke of Wellington's eventual ascendance and Napoleon's abdication. He also likened it to Vince Lombardi's great football achievements. Gingrich was feeling on top of the world. That same night one of his top lieutenants, Bob Livingston, chairman of the Appropriations Committee, returned home late as well:

> When Bob Livingston got home that night, his daughter said that someone from the White House had called. He was exhausted. They were the last people he wanted to talk to right now. But he placed the return call out of curiosity, and was told by a Clinton

aide that the president wanted to play golf with Livingston the next day. I'll have to think about that, Livingston said. A minute later he phoned back and accepted.

So there he was, still bone-tired on a Saturday morning, hacking his way from tee to green, the President of the United States serving as his chauffeur, partner, and golf teacher. Livingston had heard about Clinton's charm, but he had never seen it firsthand like this before. The president never stopped shooting the bull. He boasted about how he once outdrove Jack Nicklaus. And he was booming the ball today, too, driving it almost 250 yards straight down the fairway on many holes. "This guy is pretty good," Livingston thought to himself.

For his part, Livingston's game was falling apart. It seemed that the worse he hacked and sliced, the nicer Clinton became. Every now and then, between shots, the president talked shop. The buzz around Washington was about a potential train wreck in the fall. All those appropriation bills coming over to the White House, one less acceptable to the president than the next. No way he could sign that Labor–HHS bill that the Republicans just passed. Maybe they could work things out, do some compromising, meet the policy concerns of Clinton, and avoid the train wreck.

Thwack! Sure don't want to have to veto all those bills, said the president. *Hack!* Sure hope you don't, said Livingston, trying to keep his head down. Big Bob ended up in the rough a lot, but he went home with three presidential golf balls.

Livingston also went home with the lesson that the revolution would not be as easy as the Republicans had thought. It was August, and President Clinton was beginning to reemerge as a relevant figure in American politics. The Republicans had pushed through so much legislation in their first seven months that they almost forgot about President Clinton, but there he was, reminding Bob Livingston that if they really wanted to achieve anything in the end, they would have to deal with him.

My biography of President Clinton, *First in His Class*, provides clues as to how Clinton managed to recover from the low point of November 1994 when the Republicans won the election to the point in August when he began to reemerge. He had also rebounded from an enormous loss many years before. In 1980, after serving as governor of Arkansas for only two years, he was defeated for reelection and at age 35 was rendered the youngest ex-governor in American history. The first thing he did was to call a political consultant named Dick Morris, who was from the upper west side of New York.

Morris had helped Clinton in his first gubernatorial campaign, and he came to Arkansas to help reconstruct Clinton's political career. He told him to move to the center on all of the major issues, co-opting the Republicans wherever possible. Suddenly ex-Governor Clinton began speaking out for the first time against the death penalty, drafting proposals to reform the welfare system, and apologizing for raising taxes in Arkansas. In the 1982 gubernatorial campaign, he quickly captured the imagination of the Arkansas people once again. He asked for forgiveness, and they forgave him. Clinton was elected once again in 1982 and served as governor for the next decade.

After the Democratic party's defeat in the 1994 elections, Clinton followed the same familiar pattern. Once again he called Dick Morris, who in the meantime had been a consultant to various Republicans. Nevertheless, Morris jumped at the chance to help the President of the United States. He became a consultant for the President before anyone besides Bill and Hillary Clinton knew about it. For a while he would use pseudonyms when sending messages. Once again, he recommended to President Clinton that he move to the center whenever possible, such as on the social issues of crime and welfare, and he told Clinton to present his own version of a balanced budget. First, Clinton said he could balance the budget in ten years, then he said eight years and finally seven years, which matched the time frame that the Republicans had proposed. Morris helped position the President for a comeback during those six or seven months that the Republicans were storming through the House and Senate. He put President Clinton back in the center of things by August so that the balanced budget fight turned out to be much more of an even battle than the Republicans had anticipated.

Gingrich made a decision early on to stake the success of the Republican party's entire agenda all on one bill. All of the major reforms he sought, including reductions in the rate of growth in

Medicare and Medicaid and cuts in educational and environmental funds, depended on the massive appropriation bill that was the first step toward a balanced budget. It was an all-or-nothing gamble based on his belief that in the end, President Clinton would bow to the Republicans' will under the weight of public pressure. Under that assumption, the House Republicans began pushing their balanced budget proposal that fall in a way that gave no hint of compromise. By early November, it reached the point where they were ready to shut down the government if President Clinton did not agree to their plan for balancing the budget.

On 13 November 1995, a final meeting was held at the White House to try to reach a budget agreement to prevent an imminent government shutdown. Speaker Gingrich went into that meeting with the assumption that he and Senate Majority Leader Dole would call President Clinton's bluff and prevail. When they got to the Oval Office, however, President Clinton showed a stiff backbone that none of them had seen before. He declared to the Republican leaders that he did not care if his popularity fell to 5 percent in the polls, he would not agree to the cuts in Medicare, Medicaid, education, and the environment that the Republicans were insisting on. Even President Clinton's own aides were stunned by the strength of that speech.

After the meeting, Vice President Gore told Clinton that he should tell the American public how strongly opposed he was to the Republicans' budget plan just has he had done in the meeting but that he should say he would not change even if his popularity went down to *zero* rather than 5 percent. President Clinton put his arm around Gore and said, "No, that's not right, Al. If I go down to 4 percent, I'm caving." That night they laughed in a way that they had not been able to do in a long time.

The White House team finally did prove their relevancy in November, and the Republicans learned that the President would not capitulate. The government closed for about five days, after which a temporary agreement was reached. About a month later, the crisis erupted once again as the two sides quarreled over the definition of a balanced budget. In our book, Michael and I developed the theme that the Republicans did not know when to declare victory. They had essentially gotten the President and his people to agree to balance the budget in seven years, but then a fight erupted over whether it would be scored by the Congressional Budget Office, whose economic projections were much more conservative, or the Office of Management and Budget (part of the Executive Office of the President), which had more leeway in its numbers. The Republicans thought this issue was so important that they decided to stand their ground and fight it out. It was a critical mistake because the public did not have any knowledge of or interest in how the budget should be scored. The Republicans ended up making it merely a mathematical argument, whereas the Democrats and President Clinton could say that they too were trying to balance the budget but were not going to let the Republicans cut such important policy programs as Medicare, the environment, and education.

The Republicans were slow to catch on to this tactic, and one of the problems again was personalities. President Clinton had a remarkable capacity to overwhelm Speaker Gingrich with charm whenever they were in a room together. Although these two men differ greatly in their politics, they are alike in many ways. Clinton and Gingrich both come from somewhat dysfunctional families without strong father figures. Both had incredible political ambitions from an early age—Clinton wanted to be president from the time he was 16 years old, and Gingrich wanted to be Speaker of the House, which is an unusual desire, from the time he was in college. Both loved to talk policy and had eclectic ideas. Neither was truly an ideologue, although Speaker Gingrich sometimes appeared to be as he came up through the House ranks.

Here they were in late 1995 at the peak of their powers, both with their careers at stake. Clinton's presidency clearly was on the line; Speaker Gingrich's revolution was on the line. After meeting face-to-face for an extraordinary 50 hours, President Clinton ultimately prevailed. Gingrich claimed that Clinton had deceived him by repeatedly hinting that a deal was imminent when in reality he had no intention of making a deal. However one interprets this climactic negotiation, it is clear that the President had outfoxed the Speaker in one of the most important battles of their lives.

In the House of Representatives, meanwhile, Speaker Gingrich was really losing control. From the beginning he understood that closing down the government was a near-fatal strategic maneuver, but he could not control his own House. In the book, we documented the leadership meetings in the House in which Majority Leader Armey and many of the freshmen were chanting, "Shut it down," like radical university students of the 1960s. John Kasich said that he walked into one of the meetings and thought to himself, "My God, they're burning the furniture and they've killed the fatted calf!" In meeting after meeting, they voted to close the government, in defiance of Gingrich's recommendation. He was unable to make the House understand what was happening until after it was too late and the public relations damage had already been done.

Our book ends on 9 January 1996 with the Speaker driving back to the Capitol from the White House the night that the budget negotiations broke down. He realized that he had blundered in his most important confrontation of the year and was uncertain what to do next. We interviewed him afterward, and he said, "You can look at 1995 as the sum cost of inventing Diet Coke." Gingrich's district is near Coca-Cola headquarters, and he had spent thousands of hours studying how Coca-Cola managed its employees and adapted to change. When Diet Coke was first introduced, it was not profitable, but after a couple of years it caught on and became a big market success. Gingrich hopes the same thing will happen with his Republican revolution.

Actually, the Republicans no longer use the word *revolution* anymore. They realized that it probably overpromised what they were trying to do and it frightened people; it is now maybe a reformation at best. President Clinton now has a 16 percent advantage in the polls, and Newt Gingrich is struggling to show that *he* is relevant! Nevertheless, the cycles of modern American politics come quicker and quicker, and in the last couple of weeks President Clinton has started to slip. The next several months could be fascinating indeed.

QUESTION: Can you predict who will win the next election and which way Congress might go?

MR. MARANISS: In 1992 I made an early prediction that President Clinton would be elected president. Since I was right then, I am sure I will be wrong this time!

I think it will be an extremely close election, nowhere near the 16-to-20 percent spread in the polls that there is now. The election results may depend on what happens with the Whitewater investigation, but I do not think it will be the decisive factor unless there is a major indictment of someone in the White House. President Clinton is probably the best campaigner in modern times, and given the strong economy the United States is enjoying right now, he will probably win reelection.

There is a chance that the Democrats will retake the House, although perhaps if the public expects Clinton to win, they might vote a split ticket and allow the Republicans to retain the House. The Democrats think that they have a chance of recapturing 50 House seats, and many of those seats are definite possibilities. Even though Bob Dole has begun to separate himself from Gingrich in the "revolution," the two men are inextricably linked. Gingrich will have to find his voice again in articulating a message for the Republicans not to just hold the House, but to stay strong. Although Bob Dole has many positive attributes, he is unable to articulate a policy vision as clearly as Gingrich, notwithstanding the latter's verbal gaffes. The outcome, then, depends largely on the abilities of Speaker Gingrich and President Clinton, respectively, to stay away from trouble.

QUESTION: I was surprised that the *Washington Post* devoted four pages to a story about Hillary Clinton's legal problems yesterday. Does this mean that the editors anticipate another scandal on the scale of Watergate?

MR. MARANISS: I wrote that story. The fact that it was run has nothing to do with whether anyone at the *Washington Post* saw a parallel with Watergate. I view myself as an objective analyst and observer. There are legitimate questions that are not going away, and we were trying to study them over the four years.

Devoting so much space in the newspaper was a major commitment, and the editors spent a great deal of time thinking about how the public would interpret that action. Basically, they thought the story was worthwhile. There was certainly no political agenda on the paper's part one way or the other.

QUESTION: Some people believe that the net result of the recent budget battles will be that any truly valiant effort to touch the "third rail" of American politics—that is, reforming the entitlement programs such as Medicare and Medicaid—will be futile. Is that the case? If so, how would you assign responsibility? Is it due to the ideological extremism of the Republican freshman class or to the Democrats demagoguing the whole budget issue?

MR. MARANISS: Your assessment of this situation is exactly right. The Republicans made certain mistakes such as underestimating Clinton's resolve and denying the extent of proposed cuts during the first six months that made it much more difficult for them to make a straightforward, honest presentation to the public about how they were going to balance the budget. They appeared to be zealously cutting needed programs such as Medicare, and it hurt their public image. On the Democratic side, there are two levels to what happened. Some would say that President Clinton's sudden refusal to compromise was a purely political ploy—that once the White House realized that they were winning the message war by denouncing the major cuts that the Republicans were attempting and that it was helping them climb back into the political game, they decided to continue to demagogue it as much as possible. An argument can also be made on the policy level, but I think the political considerations were somewhat stronger. Therefore, both parties share some responsibility for the inability to deal with the "third rail."

QUESTION: How long will it take before anyone will propose reforming entitlements again? Sooner or later, something will have to be done.

MR. MARANISS: It depends somewhat on who controls the White House. If Senator Dole were elected president and the Republicans maintained control of Congress, they probably would return to those issues but not be as ambitious in attempting to tackle the problem as they were under Clinton. It is not that they will never address those issues again, but inevitably, politics will continue to get in the way.

QUESTION: How big an effect on the election would Ross Perot have if he runs on the Reform party ticket? Would it affect the Dole ticket more than the Clinton ticket?

MR. MARANISS: Studies of the 1992 election showed that President Clinton would have won even if Perot had not been a candidate. In 1995, the polls indicated that most people who identified themselves as Perot supporters were from the Republican party, implying that a Perot candidacy would have helped President Clinton immensely. A subtle shift has been occurring lately, however, and since public frustration with both parties has risen, I am not sure whether Clinton or Dole would be hurt more if Perot runs.

QUESTION: You have talked a great deal about the confrontation between Speaker Gingrich and the President. What was Majority Leader Dole's role during this time?

MR. MARANISS: From the beginning, Dole realized that he had to form an alliance with House Republicans. Thus, when the 104th Congress convened in January, Speaker Gingrich and Senator Dole began to meet almost daily to plan a joint strategy on policy. Their respective chiefs of staff did meet everyday. At times the Senate was more moderate than the House, and Dole would make a sarcastic statement criticizing the "revolutionaries." He usually alerted Gingrich before he made these statements, so it was not as much of a surprise as it appeared to be. By the time the balanced budget negotiations started, however, most of the "true revolutionaries" in the House had come to dislike Dole. Speaker Gingrich, who in the 1980s had bluntly dismissed Dole as "the tax collector for the welfare state," had grown to truly respect him, and they were actually allies in private. In public, the Republican leadership in the House was constantly criticizing Dole for being too slow and not understanding the need to act more decisively.

At one point, the House leadership was meeting, and everyone was pounding on the table and chanting, "Shut down the government." Gingrich turned to his aide, Dan Meyer, and told him to call Sheila Burke, Dole's chief of staff, and get Dole over there to see what was happening. Dole came and sat in on the House meeting, obviously not very pleased, and everyone was screaming that Clinton could not be trusted and that the government had to be shut down—who cared about the government anyway? When Dole was thanked by Gingrich for coming over, he replied, "You bet. Kinda reminded me of my days in the House over here." He was always rather low-key.

During the budget negotiations, Dole wanted to reach an agreement. He thought that if he and President Clinton had been alone in a room for an hour, they could have solved the dispute. At one point Dole and Clinton were talking on the phone about the budget shutdown and lamenting the situation in the House. President Clinton even gave Dole some campaign advice, saying that a prompt budget deal would enable Dole to devote his efforts to campaigning in New Hampshire and other states. When Clinton hung up the phone, he said to his aides, "Bob Dole, my new best friend." At times Clinton seemed like a closer ally of Dole than the House leadership.

QUESTION: I have a question about the political utility of the Contract With America. Would you comment on whether the Republicans' failure in the war over public opinion was due primarily to their tenacious attempt to carry out every last item in the Contract, or was it due, as you suggested, to their behind-the-scenes attempts to push through certain items that were not highlighted in the Contract?

MR. MARANISS: I believe the Republicans essentially misread their mandate in the November 1994 election. They thought the voters had endorsed the Contract With America, but in fact the polls show that even in April 1995 when activity related to the

Contract was at its peak, only 10 to 15 percent of the public had ever heard of it. It is hard to call that a mandate.

The elections of 1994 were an expression of public anger against Washington. Some of that anger was inchoate general frustration; some people thought there was just too much big government and too much taxation. The Republicans eagerly exerted the power they had been given after being in the minority for 40 years and quickly became embroiled in controversy. For instance, they allowed corporate lobbyists to rewrite the deregulation laws and gut the workplace safety laws. Many people felt that they were replacing big government with big business interest. They appeared to be doing business as usual, and they began to lose their momentum. Thus, it was much more difficult later for them to deal with Medicare and other changes.

QUESTION: It seems to me that the Republicans have not articulated their program clearly enough, which has enabled President Clinton to preempt many aspects of their policy. Why has this strategy gone largely unnoticed by the public?

MR. MARANISS: That problem is a constant source of frustration for the Republicans. It is always hard to separate policy from message; both are incredibly important. The Democrats beat the Republicans at the message battle last year, starting with the controversy over cuts in the school lunch program. In fact, the Republicans were *not* cutting the program; instead they were raising it, but only by 5.9 percent, which could translate into cuts in real terms after five or six years. The Democrats took hold of that issue right away and pounded at the Republicans with it. They successfully made the Republicans look like they did not care about children, and they won the message war for the rest of the year.

President Clinton's co-opting of Republican issues drove the Republicans crazy, but they were not effective in combating that strategy. They kept changing who was in charge of their communications, and as Gingrich's popularity diminished because of his own mistakes, that job became even more difficult.

QUESTION: Both the Democratic and Republican proposals to balance the budget in seven years tend to postpone making the hard choices until five, six, or seven years after the next election. Is either one of those plans better than the other? Is the most meaningful mechanism to control federal spending still George Bush's 1990 agreement that if spending is raised in one place, it must be cut in another?

MR. MARANISS: Judging whether the Democratic or the Republican budget plan is better depends on what policies you believe in. The plans put together by House Budget Committee Chairman Kasich are more brave in that cuts are to be made earlier rather than putting them all off until the sixth or seventh year. There is still a debate within the Democratic party over whether a balanced budget within seven years or even nine years is really necessary. That debate might resurface if the Democrats regain control of the House.

NARRATOR: One of Mr. Kasich's arguments is that the Republicans have made more concessions that the Democrats have. Is there any merit to that argument?

MR. MARANISS: Once the balanced-budget negotiations began, the Republicans did make many more concessions that the Democrats did. The Democrats argued, however, that by merely agreeing to a seven-year balanced budget, they had made an enormous concession; it took them to the edge of where they were willing to go in terms of policy cuts.

NARRATOR: Kasich stands out as a key player on the Republican side. Who stands out among the negotiators on the Democratic side?

MR. MARANISS: White House Chief of Staff Leon Panetta is clearly the instrumental figure—more so than anyone in Congress, although Senate Minority Leader Tom Daschle emerged as a strong figure in the final couple of months. George Stephanopoulos reemerged as a strong character in the White House because he devised the day-to-day tactics that prevailed in the war over the balanced budget. He was the one that drove the Republicans crazy.

Michael Weisskopf and I spent a great deal of time with John Kasich, and he is very bright and funny. He seemed to be an honest broker in the sense that he truly cared more about finding a way to balance the budget than in pleasing the various interest groups that were brought to bear on some other Republicans.

QUESTION: As the budget negotiations reached a climax, President Clinton was very vocal in his opposition to the Medicare cut. I think he demagogued it a bit. Even so, it seems to me that the Republicans became vulnerable very early as a result of the tax cut issue, and it was never clear to me why they persisted with that position. Would they have won the balanced-budget dispute if they had moderated their position on the tax cut?

MR. MARANISS: Yes, you are absolutely right. The Republicans' inability to separate the tax cuts from their proposal to reform Medicare lost it for them right at the beginning. From the moment that they proposed a budget where the size of the tax cuts was about the same as the amount they wanted to cut Medicare, they lost the public forever. It seemed obvious to the public that the tax cut was directly related to the proposed cuts in projected growth rates in Medicare. The Republicans have begun to push for another tax cut, although I did notice that William Archer, the chairman of the Ways and Means Committee, was cautioning them against proposing a major tax cut on the grounds that it would lead to another public relations disaster.

QUESTION: What is the division of labor between you and Michael Weisskopf?

MR. MARANISS: He and I began working at the *Washington Post* during the same week 19 years ago. We reported on Maryland politics together, and we covered the trial of Marvin Mandel when he was governor and the Maryland State House under Harry Hughes. Michael is one of the finest reporters in Washington, with expert knowledge of the connections between lobbyists and political players. I was familiar with the major players, so our labor was divided more or less along those lines.

NARRATOR: We have been privileged to hear David Maraniss again. We are grateful to him for sharing a portion of his vast accumulation of information about the debt and the deficit.